SOCIAL CLASS AND
THE COMPREHENSIVE SCHOOL

Social Class
and the
Comprehensive School

JULIENNE FORD

LONDON
ROUTLEDGE & KEGAN PAUL

First published in 1969
by Routledge & Kegan Paul Limited
Broadway House, 68–74 Carter Lane, London EC4V 5EL
Reprinted 1972
Printed in Great Britain by
Redwood Press Limited
© J. B. Ford 1969

ISBN 0 7100 6579 5 (c)
ISBN 0 7100 7481 6 (p)

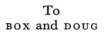

To
BOX and DOUG

Preface

Unless the value relevances of sociological inquiry are made plainly evident, unless there are at least some bridges between it and larger human hopes and purposes, it must inevitably be scorned by laymen as pretentious and word-mongering. But the manner in which some sociologists conceive the value-free doctrine disposes them to ignore current human problems and to huddle together like old men seeking warmth. 'This is not our job,' they say, 'and if it were we would not know enough to do it. Go away, come back when we are grown up,' say these old men. The issue, however, is not whether we know enough; the real questions are whether we have the courage to say and use what we do know and whether anyone knows more.[1]

A recent investigation by the British Sociological Association revealed that the most rapidly expanding sociological specialism is education. Yet, while hundreds of works in this field are published annually, sociologists have made practically no contribution to actual policy decisions about education. Major changes in educational policy continue to be made without the benefit of the knowledge which sociologists could provide. The sociologists turn their backs and continue 'doing the easy thing because it is accurate and avoiding the difficult thing because it is imprecise'.[2]

Meanwhile it has been decided that what is needed, as a first step towards the 'Fairer Society', is comprehensive reorganization of secondary education. No one knows quite what will happen. But it is generally felt that the situation couldn't be worse. As we cannot *predict* what will happen to one variable (the class system) when we manipulate another (the educational system), why not just do it and see? The effect is a gigantic

[1] Alvin Gouldner 'Anti-Minotaur: The Myth of a Value-Free Sociology' in Stein, Maurice, and Vidich, Arthur, *Sociology on Trial*, Prentice-Hall, N.J., 1963, p. 43.
[2] Nettl, J. P., *Political Mobilization: A Sociological Analysis of Methods and Concepts*, Faber and Faber, 1967.

experiment with the life chances of millions of children; and the results will not be known for years.

It is my aim in this volume to apply the limited sociological tools which *are* available to explore the reasoning behind the notion that comprehensive reform will produce the 'Fairer Society', and investigate the empirical validity of the assumptions involved. This is not a problem which readily lends itself to research. In the first place no one has actually stated the propositions of the theory from which the notion that comprehensive schooling will produce a better world is derived. Secondly, the concepts involved – for example those of *talent*, *equality of opportunity*, *class consciousness* and so on – are particularly difficult to translate into operational terms and measure. Finally, most educational research is threatened by the fact that there are a vast number of confounding variables to be controlled, and an even greater number which cannot be controlled. This operates to reduce the certainty with which inferences about causation – and hence policy conclusions – can be drawn.

The theory which I attack in this book cannot, therefore, be said to have been decisively discredited. Nor can I claim value-freedom for this work. In fact I would not want to do so. For it is in precisely those areas in which sociological research is most vital that the sociologist's own values are most likely to influence his research interests. The research problem itself, and my approach to it, have certainly been shaped by my values. So, rather than allowing this bias to sneak up on the reader in an underhand manner, I should state my position at the outset.[1] I am a socialist. Like many of the proponents of comprehensive reform I hope for the eventual destruction of the system of stratification which exists in contemporary Britain. Yet this work is intended to throw doubt on the assumption that comprehensive reorganization of secondary education will achieve this aim.

[1] It was Gunnar Myrdal who first suggested that, rather than attempting to ignore the problem of values in sociology, the author should make his own moral position explicit. See *An American Dilemma*, Harper, 1944.

Contents

Acknowledgements

I owe thanks to a large number of people without whose help this work would probably not have been completed. In particular I am grateful to David Baillie, Steven Box, and Judith Lay for assistance in computation and interpretation of the data. And I wish especially to thank Frank Parkin and David Morgan who patiently read and criticized each chapter, providing many valuable corrections and additions.

It is impossible to identify all my many intellectual creditors, however three of my friends and colleagues have made a special contribution. Despite our profound political disagreements, the influence of George Homans can be detected in many places, and I recall with affection the part he played in shaping the perspective employed in this work. I also owe a special debt to Steven Box and Douglas Young whose ideas initially inspired this research and who have been a continual source of help and inspiration ever since.

Finally I should like to thank the children and teachers in the three schools mentioned whose good humour turned what could have been a burden into quite an adventure!

Justice and the Comprehensive Ideal

Among parents and teachers, as well as Labour Party idealists and educationalists, discontent with the tripartite organization of secondary education in England and Wales is very evident. But criticism of the present system of selection does not stem so much from a rejection of the general principle whereby rewards, material and symbolic, are unequally distributed in society, as from a distaste for the current bases of discrimination. Thus, as Pedley puts it, 'The Englishman of the 1960s does not believe in equality. What he wants is equal opportunity to be unequal.'[1] On closer examination, however, even the argument for equality of *opportunity* is seen to be a cover for a yet more limited plea. For, as Benn and Peters have noted, the cry for equality of opportunity refers in practice to the desire to accord individuals the same opportunities 'only in the sense that they are all entitled to be treated alike until *relevant* grounds are established for treating them differently'.[2] In the English situation relevant grounds are almost invariably considered in the context of ability. Thus we can see the main body of current criticism of the tripartite system of education, in sociological as well as political and administrative circles, as stemming from the view that selection should be based on the sole criterion of 'ability'[3] and that this cannot be adequately ascertained by an examination at Eleven-Plus.[4]

Now it should be made clear immediately that this is always an ideological position, a bid to remove an injustice, a statement that discrimination is being made on irrelevant grounds and that this should be replaced by efficient selection on relevant and reasonable criteria.[5] Sometimes the ideological flavour of such a criticism is disguised in a variant of the functionalist view. For example, Floud and Halsey[6] argue that 'the efficient division of the working population requires both that there should be the right numbers of workers in each occupation and that the qualities of workers in each occupation should be as appropriate as possible – in short that "ability" and "opportunity" should be matched as closely as possible.'[7] They claim that under the present system this requirement is not being met adequately, and that a closer adherence to this ideal could be attained by comprehensive reorganization. Yet on closer inspection this argument is not entirely convincing. Floud and Halsey may consider the present system to be unjust, but they have not demonstrated that it is inefficient.

Consider, for example, the situation where the proportion of individuals with abilities relevant to high status jobs exceeds the number of those jobs. In this case, so long as all those who actually attain high status jobs do have the requisite abilities, 'the efficient division of the working population' is effected – but some individuals with the 'ability' to become brain surgeons have to be content with sweeping roads. Furthermore, the actual brain surgeons could have been selected from the universe of potential brain surgeons on entirely ascriptive, that is 'unreasonable', grounds; but the requirements of efficiency in the division of labour would not be threatened so long as they could actually function adequately as brain surgeons. There is no reason to assume that roadsweepers of brain-surgeon capacity would be inefficient at sweeping roads. Nor does it salvage the argument to introduce the idea of 'wastage of ability'; for, while the supply of skills or potential skills in the population exceeds the demand for such skills which is generated by the occupational structure, there will always be 'wastage of ability' regardless of the mode of selection through education.[8]

So, rather than wasting intellectual effort in attempts to rationalize ideological commitments and to present the conclusions from normative assumptions as though they were derived from value-neutral deductions, it is clearly more economic to state these value assumptions in explicit form.[9] Let us recognize that, in our discussions of the processes of educational and occupational selection, it is justice which is at issue, not efficiency. There is no fear that by formulating the argument in these terms we are relegating it to idealists and politicians; such a discussion does not lie outside the province of sociology, for our ideas about justice in general, and our mobility ideologies in particular, are important aspects of our culture which themselves merit study.

There are two opposed approaches to the study of justice among sociologists: one empirical, the other moral. The empirical position is exemplified in the work of Homans.[10] For Homans' norms of justice are determined by the empirical conditions of exchange in social relationships; 'what *is* determines what always *ought* to be.'[11] Thus what a man expects, what he considers just, is determined by his actual experience: he comes to learn that generally it happens that rewards are proportional to costs: 'if one man is "better" than another in his investments, he should also be "better" than the other in the value of the contribution he makes and in the reward he gets for it.'[12] Thus an empirical expectation, a conception of *probability*, gives rise to a normative expectation, a conception of what *ought* to be done.[13] This can be expressed by the more general Aristotelian notion that 'if (a man) is better on one count, he ought to be better on both: his rankings on the two counts should be in line with one another'.[14] On the empirical view, then, justice is a matter of expectations and the sense of injustice is aroused when expectations are defeated.[15]

The empirical approach has been attacked by Runciman[16] who, drawing on Benn and Peters,[17] stresses that just differentials in rewards are based, not on *any* differences in status or investment, but on *relevant* differences. Runciman's personal sense of justice is outraged by the denial of reward to an individual in one of Homans' examples[18] on grounds he does not see to be relevant. 'By normal standards of justice,' says Runciman, 'this is transparently unfair.'[19] But what are 'normal' standards of justice? Clearly, if we understand 'normal' in the statistical rather than the clinical sense, there is the possibility that what other people consider to be just, what is normal to a particular culture or subculture, is 'transparently unfair' to Runciman. Of course the bases of discrimination must be relevant in some sense to the discrimination in question before a difference in reward is described as just. But what are the criteria of relevance? Runciman seems to consider that there are absolute criteria which must be obvious to all reasonable men. Yet even if we were to accept this philosophically intuitionist position[20] we would still be left with the task of explaining

3

what actually happens in the world. For these purposes Runciman's personal conception of what kinds of differences between human beings are relevant bases of differential reward is of no interest; we are asking, rather, what criteria of differentiation are popularly held to be relevant to differences in reward. Thus the moral conception of justice is antipathetic to sociological explanation since conceptions of what the standards of justice ought to be are irrelevant to an understanding of the views of justice which people in fact hold.

Curiously Runciman's own *Relative Deprivation and Social Justice*[21] provides a most enlightening explanation of the way in which popular conceptions of justice actually change based on the very idea of status inconsistency which is so central to the Homansian approach to justice. Basically his argument is that 'objective' inequalities in life-chances of all kinds – the sorts of situations which liberal sociologists might describe as 'transparently unfair' – are not themselves sufficient to produce a sense of injustice in the deprived individuals. The intervening variable is the notion of *relative deprivation*.[22] Relative deprivation arises when individuals perceive inequalities between their positive reference groups and their membership groups.[23] For example, when individuals are placed in marginal positions,[24] one attribute or status making them eligible for membership in a more highly valued group in which they are not wholly accepted while other attributes assign them more firmly to a less highly valued group, they will feel relatively deprived. The debilities ascribed to them because of their membership of the less highly valued group will now come to be defined as intolerable and unjust. Thus in societies where there is a high degree of status crystallization,[25] where individuals' rankings on the various hierarchies of prestige, power, wealth, race and so on tend to be highly correlated, relative deprivation, and hence the sense of injustice, will tend to be low. On the other hand in societies undergoing more rapid social change, where mobility between statuses is greater and where consequently there is a low degree of status crystallization, there will tend to be groups and individuals who are continually redefining traditional conceptions of justice, and rejecting as unfair what was formerly accepted as right.

We have seen that our ideas about equality of educational

opportunity are aspects of our more general cultural conceptions about justice, and that changing ideas of justice in society can be explained with reference to the ideas of status crystallization and relative deprivation. We are now in a position to examine changing conceptions of justice in the sphere of education in terms of this explanatory framework.

Changing attitudes to education can be seen as changing ideas of what are *just* bases for educational discrimination. The sense of injustice arises because the sorts of differences between individuals which have been determining their educational opportunity are now seen as irrelevant. Thus the charter of the Butler Act of 1944 was to neutralize the impact of wealth on educational attainment as wealth came to be an unacceptable determinant of educational success. However the Act did not remove, nor was it designed to remove, differentials in educational opportunity, for educational chances were now to be determined by measured intelligence, and since this attribute was considered to be relevant to educational success, this new discrimination was seen to be just.

Now, while it is true that there has been some disquiet deriving from the suspicion that the Eleven-Plus test is not an accurate measure of innate intelligence,[26] it is generally agreed that this test is the best instrument yet devised to measure 'intelligence' and that alternative attempts at selection for secondary school, such as teachers' recommendations are less 'fair'.[27] How is it then that people have come to define the present system of educational selection as unjust? Their sense of injustice stems from a redefinition of 'intelligence-as-measured-by-Eleven-Plus-tests' as an irrelevant basis of discrimination. And their argument is that a new and just differentiation should be on the basis of 'real ability' rather than measured intelligence.[28]

The explanation of this changing conception of educational justice must be sought in the conditions which gave rise to a sense of relative deprivation among those not favoured by the tripartite system. It is the working class which is, and always has been, most educationally deprived.[29] But, as we have seen, deprivation is not in itself sufficient to produce the sense of relative deprivation. Since the majority of secondary modern school children have always been from working-class homes and their low educational status, and consequent low anticipations of occupational status, have been quite in accord with their parents' occupational prestige, we would not expect them or their parents to define their circumstances as unjust. This *consistently* deprived group then is not a likely source of the pressure for change; our search for an explanation of the innovation in educational attitudes becomes the search for a *marginal* group: a group with inconsistent status rankings.

When we consider the effects of the post-war 'Bulge' in the birth rate a possible answer suggests itself. The first wave of the Bulge reached the age of eleven in 1957 but there was no substantial increase in the number of places available in grammar schools. This had a two-fold impact on the intake of the secondary modern schools: they began to receive more middle-class pupils and more pupils of higher than average ability than had formerly been the case. For the first time then middle-class families, in relatively substantial numbers, were experiencing the effects of having one or more children receiving an 'inferior' education, and one which was not generally intended as a preparation for middle-class occupations. This situation of status inconsistency may well have resulted in a feeling of relative deprivation among these families, and eventually this rather vocal section of society may have come to define as unjust a system of education where children are almost certainly doomed to low status jobs by the failure of an examination at the age of eleven.

At the same time the addition of relatively able pupils to the secondary modern school may have been working in another way to introduce discontent with the system. For it has been argued[30] that headmasters of secondary modern schools took advantage of this opportunity to distinguish their schools in public examinations, entering more and more pupils for 'O' level G.C.E.[31] In 1954 the number of secondary modern schools entering pupils for G.C.E. was only 357; this figure had risen to over 1,350 by 1959 – over one-third of all secondary modern schools. The growing demand for qualifications is probably reflected in the increasing percentage of pupils staying for a fifth year in secondary modern schools. Dent notes that this rose from 3·5 per cent in 1949 to 7 per cent in 1959,[32] and by

6

1964 the proportion had reached about one in ten.[33] Thus a further source of criticism of Eleven-Plus selection is suggested. Growing awareness that some pupils, though rejected by the Eleven-Plus were capable of G.C.E. success may have led to a suspicion that this examination was somehow an inaccurate measure of 'ability'. Thus in two ways the effects of the Bulge may have operated to thwart individuals' expectations in the field of education and hence to produce a feeling of injustice resulting in rising criticism of the tripartite organization of secondary education.

So far we have considered only the negative side of our changing attitudes about education: the redefinition of tripartite education as unjust. The other aspect of current educational thought is, of course, the advocacy of comprehensive education as an alternative, which, it is believed, will abolish the unjust features of the present system and hence produce the 'Fairer Society.'

There is fairly general support for the idea of comprehensive education in this country. A recent opinion poll carried out by *New Society* and Research Services produced the following distribution of responses to the question 'Are you in favour or against comprehensive education?'[34]

TABLE I
*Social class**

	AB	C_1	C_2	DE	all	N = 1331
% In favour	46	51	58	51	52	
Don't know	17	29	27	38	29	
Against	37	20	15	11	19	

* Standard Market Research categories.

There is then substantial acceptance of comprehensive education across all social classes. Rejection, however, is clearly related to social class, for, while in the AB category only 9 per cent more accept than reject, in the DE category the difference between acceptance and rejection is 40 per cent ($p = 0.001$). Members of the social class categories who might be seen as having most to lose by comprehensive reorganization favour this policy significantly less than members of those which are seen to have most to gain. Attitudes to comprehensive education were also shown by the survey to be related to political party allegiance, 60 per cent of Labour Party, 55 per cent of Liberal Party, but only 45 per cent of Conservative Party supporters expressing acceptance of comprehensive education $(p = 0.001)$.[35]

So support for comprehensive reorganization of secondary education, while not homogenous, is fairly general and such reorganization is the expressed policy of the political party which forms the present government.[36] Yet there has been very little research into the effects of comprehensive schools,[37] and even less into the question as to the extent to which they can be expected to produce the 'Fairer Society', an expectation which is arguably the basic rationale behind this reorganization.

In order to examine this question empirically it is first necessary to clarify the precise theory on which the hypothesis *Comprehensive schools will tend to produce the 'Fairer Society'* is based. At this point the discussion turns from popular attitudes about comprehensive schools to the published literature on the subject. For there is, of course, no reason to suppose that 'the-man-in-the-street' has explicitly formulated ideas about the relationship between education and 'equality', although aspects of the more academic discussion on the matter may filter into his consciousness through the media of opinion leaders.[38]

If one turns to the published work of the advocates of comprehensive schools, any hope of discovering this theory is, however, soon disappointed. The connection between comprehensive education and the 'Fairer Society' is nowhere made clear, in fact it is often taken to be self-evident, and the connection is considered to be so obvious that no explanation is required. Thus, for example, Armstrong and Young in their Fabian pamphlet[39] assume that comprehensive schools will produce a better society, and merely discuss the various alternatives within the broad comprehensive ideal. Floud and Halsey also advocate comprehensive reorganization, with the proviso that this would produce the desired results 'only if the spirit as well as the form of English secondary education were changed,'[40] yet their reasoning is entirely based on criticism of the tripartite system.

However, while I have not found a complete theory of the effects of comprehensive schooling in any single work, it is possible to build up a sort of *ideal type* theory from the suggestions in the various sources. Such a theory, of course, will never conform completely to the views of any one author, but it should be a reasonable representation of the general line of thought which is current.

The key to the theoretical link between the tripartite system and the 'Unfair Society' seems to lie in the idea of early selection. Few critics reject selection *per se* however, their objections are specifically to *early* and relatively final differentiation on the basis of measured intelligence. Taylor, for example, argues that

if we no longer possess a criterion that will legitimize early selection, allocation and the subsequent differentiation attendant upon them, then it becomes morally imperative to shift the basis of allocation procedures from performance in intelligence and attainment tests and response to primary schooling to a more flexible procedure operating within secondary and post-secondary education, where the range of choices available is such as to make it easier for child, parent and teacher to match interests and attainments and a suitable type of course.[41]

This rejection of early selection is very often accompanied by a rejection of traditional forms of streaming as bases for grouping within the new comprehensive schools. Many writers advocate, and some schools operate, methods of breaking up the school on horizontal lines, not in any way related to academic performance, such as house systems. For it is clear that a rigid system of streaming in comprehensive schools amounts to tripartite differentation with the sole exception that grammar, technical and secondary modern schools are housed in one building. Nevertheless completely unstreamed comprehensive schools are rare and it does seem to be government policy to pursue the comprehensive ideal to its logical conclusion.[42] Thus Crosland has said, 'Both common sense and American experience suggest that (unstreaming) would lead to a really serious levelling down of standards and a quite excessive handicap to the clever child. Division into streams according to ability, remains essential,'

9

and in a footnote he adds, 'some (enthusiasts) their heads perhaps a little turned by too much sociology, even insist on classes being not known by numbers but by the teachers' names lest any mark at all of superior or inferior status be conferred. This is simply egalitarianism run mad!'[43] Where unstreaming does not accompany comprehensive organization the principle of abolition of early selection is often claimed to be protected by the fact that mobility between streams within one school is easier than mobility between schools.

Having identified the major variable in the theory which our ideal-typical advocate of comprehensives might put forward, it is now necessary to spell out the remaining intervening variables and the relationships between them. The actual arrangement of propositions in a theory is, of course, a creative business, very much a personal, even artistic endeavour. Two theorists approaching the same problem from similar perspectives could never produce the same theory, just as two painters from the same school could not, without collaboration, paint substantially similar portraits of one woman. Thus the deductive scheme suggested below, while inspired by the arguments which can be found in the literature, does not spring directly from those arguments. It is, like all ideal types, an imaginative reconstruction, a product of selective emphasis and exaggeration.

THE THEORY

Proposition One   Early selection of children into groups with differential educational and occupational prospects

(i)   prevents the fullest development of talent,
(ii)   inhibits equality of educational opportunity for those with equal talent,
(iii) prematurely confines children's occupational horizons,
(iv)   segregates potential occupational 'successes' from 'failures', hence echoing and reinforcing the system of stratification in the wider society.

Proposition Two   Where conditions (iii) and (iv) occur children's perceptions of the structure and meaning of stratification tend to take the form of rigid dichotomous models.

Proposition Three   Where (iii) and (iv) do not occur children's perceptions of the structure and meaning of stratification tend to take the form of flexible hierarchic models.

Proposition Four   Under a tripartite system of secondary education early selection of children into groups with differential educational and occupational prospects is present.

Proposition Five   Under a comprehensive system of secondary education early selection does not occur to such a great extent.

Proposition Six   Movement from a tripartite to a comprehensive organisation of secondary education will therefore cause

(*a*)   a greater development of talent,
(*b*)   a greater equality of opportunity for those with equal talent,
(*c*)   a widening of children's occupational horizons,
(*d*)   a relative decline in the social interaction in school which takes place within the boundaries of anticipated occupational strata, and a relative increase in interaction across such strata.

Proposition Seven   Conditions (*c*) and (*d*) will produce a tendency to greater frequency of flexible hierarchic models of stratification over rigid dichotomous models.

None of these propositions is inherently untestable; however, I will be concerned with testing only propositions six and seven, as any refutation of these would be sufficient to throw doubt upon the whole theory. Naturally the theory would be even more fundamentally questioned if the fifth proposition were to prove false. While this has not been specifically tested there is sufficient evidence available to give strong grounds for *suspecting* it to be false. Studies of the determinants of educational success in primary schools[44] suggest that academic successes and failures are largely selected long before the stage of entry to secondary school, and it might be argued that, for this reason, reform of secondary education is irrelevant. However for present purposes it will be assumed that there is less early selection under comprehensive educational schemes. The implications of making this assumption for the purposes of testing the theory will be discussed more fully in Chapter 7.

Returning to the sixth and final propositions we see that these two statements suggest five hypotheses:

1 Comprehensive schools will produce a greater development of talent than tripartite schools.
2 Comprehensive schools will provide greater equality of opportunity for those with equal talent.
3 The occupational horizons of children in comprehensive schools will be widened relative to those of children in tripartite schools.
4 Comprehensive school children will show less tendency to mix only with children of their own social type than will tripartite school children.
5 Comprehensive school children will tend to have views of the class system as a flexible hierarchy, while tripartite school children will tend to see this as a rigid dichotomy.

Hypothesis One The idea that early selection prevents the fullest development of talent derives from a rejection of the notion that ability is a fixed genetic quality, a notion that was behind the provisions of the 1944 Act. Burt, in his report to the Consultative Committee in 1931 stated, 'Before this age (12) is reached children need to be grouped according to their capacity, not merely in separate classes or standards but in separate types of school.'[45] The similar argument put forward in the Norwood Report, that the three types of schools were designed to cater for three types of minds, is by now infamous.[46] Against this the argument has recently been advanced that the attainment of different standards by children selected for different types of education is no more than a self-fulfilling prophecy: that children do as well as they *think* they can and their perceptions are shaped by the way the educational system defines them.[47] In fact, as will be explained in *Chapter 2*, there is as yet no definite empirical evidence in support of this argument. However, in so far as it is now widely believed that talent is produced by school experience rather than given exclusively by birth, then norms of equality will be concerned with the provision of equal opportunity for each individual to *develop* his talent to the full, rather than the more limited notion of equal opportunity for those with equal talent.[48]

Hypothesis Two The more limited notion that early selection actually inhibits equality of educational opportunity for those with equal talent is a common one. This will be discussed in *Chapter 3*, where evidence from a sample of fourteen and fifteen year olds in tripartite and comprehensive schools will be brought to bear on the question whether or not comprehensive schooling increases the possibility that equal opportunities will be available to children of equal talent.

Hypothesis Three Another aspect of the self-fulfilling prophecy notion as it relates to early selection is contained in the idea that different types of school 'feed' different occupations, not only because of the differences in the actual educational content provided – an effect specifically fashioned by the Butler Act – but also because of children's definitions of their ability. Research in England and Scotland has demonstrated the way in which type of school determines children's occupational horizons relative to their parents. Working-class boys in a London grammar school were found to have 'unrealistically' high expectations of social mobility[49] while secondary modern school children were found to set their sights 'realistically' low.[50] In *Chapter 4* occupational plans and aspirations of children in tripartite and secondary modern schools will be examined and compared in an attempt to test the hypothesis that comprehensive schooling effects a widening of occupational horizons.

Hypothesis Four It is a well documented fact that, in schools with early selection, friendships within school tend to occur among children of similar social-class background, and tend also to be confined to children with similar educational and occupational prospects.[51] However, no study has been published which tests the hypothesis that comprehensive schooling will reduce these effects, thus undermining the way in which school experience reinforces the class structure. This hypothesis will be examined in *Chapter 5* where the attempt to undermine vertical stratification by breaking up the school into horizontal house groups will also be discussed.

Hypothesis Five In *Chapter 6* the way in which perceptions of social stratification are related to educational experience will be discussed and a typology of stratification maps suggested. The specific hypothesis that children who have experienced comprehensive schooling will be less likely to hold rigid dichotomous models of social class than tripartite school children will then be tested.

NOTES

1 Pedley, Robin, *The Comprehensive School*, Pelican, Penguin, 1963, p. 11.
2 Benn, S. I., and Peters, R. S., *Social Principles and the Democratic State*, Allen & Unwin, 1959.
3 The relationship between the concept of 'ability' and that of 'intelligence' will be examined and discussed in *Chapter 2*.
4 A common theme in such criticisms concerns the plight of the late developer, prematurely abandoned by tripartite but encouraged to attain his maximum potential in the comprehensive school.
5 Thus in the Labour Party Manifesto *Signposts for the Sixties*, London, 1961, we read: 'To achieve genuine equality of educational opportunity we require . . . to reorganise the State secondary schools on comprehensive lines, in order to end the segregation by the Eleven-Plus examination which is now almost universally condemned on educational as well as social grounds.' A similar argument appears in Crosland, C. A. R., *The Future of Socialism*, Jonathan Cape, London, 1956.
6 Floud, Jean, and Halsey, A. H., 'English Secondary Schools and the Supply of Labour', in Halsey, A. H., Floud, J., and Anderson, C.A., *Education, Economy, and Society*, Free Press, 1961, pp. 80–92.
7 *Ibid*, p. 80. Note the similarity here to the argument of Davis, K., and Moore, W. E., 'Some Principles of Stratification', *Amer. Soc. Rev.*, X (1945), pp. 242–9.
8 This line of argument is somewhat similar to that advanced against the functionalist theory of stratification by Buckley who points out that the functionalist approach leaves out the whole question of how individuals get into positions in the occupational structure, i.e., it confuses an epidemiological with an aetiological level of analysis. See Buckley, W., 'Social Stratification and the Functionalist Theory of Social Differentiation', *American Soc. Rev.*, XXIII (1958), pp. 369–75.

9 A celebrated exponent of this idea is Gunnar Myrdal. See his 'The Relation Between Social Theory and Social Policy', *Brit. Journ. Sociol.*, XXIII (1953), pp. 210–42; *Value in Social Theory*, New York, 1958, and *An American Dilemma*, Harper, 1944.

10 The major argument is presented in Homans, G. C., *Social Behaviour: Its Elementary Forms*, Routledge, 1961, pp. 232–64.

11 Homans, G. C. 'Fundamental Social Processes' in Smelser, N. J., *Sociology*, Wiley, 1967, p. 64.

12 Homans, *op. cit.* (1961), p. 245.

13 For an interesting discussion of the distinction between 'ought's of empirical and normative expectations' see Gross, N., Mason, N. S., and McEachern, A. W., *Explorations in Role Analysis*, Wiley, 1958, Chapter 4.

14 Homans, *op. cit.* (1967), pp. 64–5. See also Aristotle, *Nichomachean Ethics*, Book V, Chapters 3 and 4. Homans notes also the similarity to Jouvenel's 'What men find just is to preserve between themselves, as regards whatever is in question, the same relations that exist between them as regards anything else'; *op. cit.* (1961), p. 245.

15 For other discussions of the empirical conception of justice and its relationship to social exchange see Blau, P. M., *Exchange and Power in Social Life*, Wiley, 1964, especially pp. 156–8 and 228; and Ford, Julienne, *et. al.*, 'Functional Autonomy, Role Distance and Social Class', *Brit. Journ. Sociol*, XVIII (4) (1967), pp. 370–81. Both these stress norms of justice as aspects of culture deriving from patterns of social exchange. See also the interesting phenomenological approach to ideas of equality in Schutz, Alfredo, *Collected Papers*, Vol. II, Nijhoff, Hague, 1964, especially pp. 239–44, and 257–73.

16 Runciman, W. G., 'Justice, Congruence and Professor Homans', *Archiv. Europ, Sociol.*, VIII (1967), pp. 115–28.

17 *Op. cit.*

18 This example was taken from Whyte, W. F., *Street Corner Society*, Chicago University Press, 1943. Whyte noted that Alec, who had low status in the gang failed to do well in bowling tournaments between all members of the gang, although his performance in friendly matches indicated that his bowling skill was quite high.

19 *Op. cit.*, p. 118.

20 Runciman's philosophical intuitionism draws heavily on the work of John Rawls. Very briefly the argument is that fairness could be intuited by rational and impartial men if they were required to agree on principles by which they would be pre-

pared to make and concede claims. As Runciman puts it, 'To make a claim on the basis of justice, therefore, is not merely to claim what is seen as a right, but to claim what is a right only if it derives from a *principle* to which the claimant could have subscribed before knowing whether he might not be the loser, rather than the gainer, by the acceptance of it', *op. cit.*, p. 253. See Rawls' three articles, 'Justice as Fairness', *Philosophical Review*, LXVII (1958), pp. 164–94; 'The Sense of Justice', Ibid., LXXII (1963), pp. 281–305; and 'Constitutional Liberty and the Concept of Justice', *Nomos*, VI (1963), pp. 98–125.

21 Routledge, 1966.

22 This concept was first introduced by Stouffer, S. A., *et. al.*, *The American Soldier*, Vol. I, Princeton Univ. Press, 1949. See also the experimental demonstration of the relative deprivation hypothesis in Spector, A. J., 'Expectations, fulfilment and morale', *J. Abnorm. Soc. Psychol.*, LII (1956), pp. 51–6.

23 Runciman distinguishes between three types of reference groups: membership, comparative and normative (*op. cit.*, pp. 9–16). However this is a little confusing as the types are not mutually exclusive. It is perhaps more enlightening for this discussion to think in terms of a two-dimensional typology. Any particular group to which any specific individual refers may be classified according firstly to whether or not he is *accepted* as a member of it, and secondly to his *evaluation* of membership of it.

	accepted into group	not accepted into group
positively evaluates membership	1	2
negatively evaluates membership	3	4

It is, then, the feeling which arises when an individual compares a group of Type 2 with one of Type 3 which is described as relative deprivation.

This typology does not in any way exhaust the meaningful distinctions which can be made between different types of reference groups; for example, some groups provide normative standards for their members while others do not, in addition one could distinguish between reference groups according to their saliency for the individuals involved. For a fuller understanding of the concept of reference group than can be provided here, the reader should consult Kelley, H. H., 'Two Functions of Reference Groups' in Swanson, G. H., *et. al.*, *Readings in Social Psychology*, 2nd edn.; N.Y., 1952, pp. 410–14; and Linn, Erwin L., 'Reference Group: A Case Study in Conceptual Diffusion', *Sociological Quarterly* (1964), 5, pp. 489–99, where a summary of the previous literature is provided.

24 For definitions of the concept of marginality and summaries of the vast literature on the subject see Dickie-Clark, H. F., *The Marginal Situation*, Routledge, 1966, and Box, Steven, and Ford, Julienne, 'Commitment to Science; A Solution to Student Marginality?', *Sociology*, 1(3) (1967), pp. 225–38.

25 The concept of status crystallization was recently popularized by Lenski, Gerhard, see for example his 'Status crystallization: A Non-Vertical Dimension of Social Status', *Amer. Soc. Rev.*, XIX (1954), p. 405. However the concept is by no means a new one and there are a multitude of terminological synonyms. The major alternative terms are *Status Consistency* probably first used by Kenkel, W. F., 'The Relationship between Status Consistency and Politico-Economic Attitudes', *loc. cit.*, XXI, 4 (1956), pp. 365–8; *'Goodness of Fit'*, which is used by Broom who clearly differentiates between crystallization on macro and micro levels – a distinction ignored by some of the writers above, see 'Social Differentiation and Stratification' in Merton, Robert K., Broom, Leonard, and Cottrell, Leonard. *Sociology Today*, Harper, 1959. An earlier usage is to be found in Benoit-Smullyan's introduction of the concept of *Status Equilibration*, which refers to the process of adjusting the lower to the higher status; Benoit-Smullyan E. 'Status, Status Types and Status Interrelationships', *Amer. Soc. Rev.* 9 (1944), pp. 151–61. The earliest version, however, is probably Parsons' *Vagueness of Class Structure* in his 1940 essay 'An Analytical Approach to the Theory of Social Stratification', in Parsons, Talcott, *Essays in Sociological Theory*, Free Press, 1964, pp. 69–88.

26 The Crowther Report found that nearly one-third of the R.A.F. recruits' performances in their I.Q. tests on entering the service indicated that they had had the 'wrong' type of schooling: *15 to 18*, Vol. 1, H.M.S.O. (1959), p. 72.

27 See Yates, A., and Pidgeon, D. A., 'Transfer at Eleven-Plus' *Educational Research*, 1 (1958), p. 13. See also Floud and Halsey's comparison of 'class chances' of entry to grammar school in an L.E.A. operating teacher recommendation in 'Social Class,

Intelligence Tests, and Selection for Secondary Schools', Halsey *et. al.*, *op. cit.* (1961), pp. 209–15.

28 The notion that measured intelligence is not an epistemic correlate of 'real ability' will be discussed in *Chapter Two*.

29 For two excellent studies of the formidable number of separate pieces of evidence on this issue see Elder, Glen, 'Life Opportunities and Personality: Some Consequences of Stratified Secondary Education in Great Britain', *Sociology of Education*, XXXVIII (3) (1965), pp. 173–202; and Little, A., and Westergaard, J., 'The Trend of Class Differentials in Educational Opportunity', *Brit. Journ. Sociol.*, XV (1964), pp. 301–15.

30 Box, Steven, and Young, Douglas, 'Reform of Secondary Education in Britain', unpublished monograph, The Polytechnic, London (1963).

31 See Taylor, William, *The Secondary Modern School*, Faber, 1963, also the Beloe Report, H.M.S.O. (1960). Of course similar pressures may also have been coming from secondary school teachers. For, once the syllabus of the modern school began to resemble that of the grammar school, their personal chances of career mobility were increased.

32 Dent, H. C., *The Educational System of England and Wales*, London, U.L.P., 1961.

33 Rough estimate based on the number of children leaving school at age 16 or later, *Educational Statistics* (1964).

34 From Dennison, D. V., 'Education and Opinion', *New Society*, 26 October (1967).

35 This finding is, however, probably on artifact of social class which was not simultaneously controlled.

36 Of course this does not mean that comprehensive reorganization had not got under way before the election of a Labour government. For the progress made up to 1963, see Pedley, *op. cit.*

37 Most of the research available has taken the form of impressionistic surveys such as Miller, T. W. G., *Values in the Comprehensive School*, Oliver and Boyd, 1961, and Currie, K., 'A study of the English Comprehensive School system with particular reference to the educational, social and cultural effects of single sex and co-educational types of school' Ph.D. (Ed.), London (1962).

38 See Katz, Elihu, and Lazarsfeld, Paul F., *Personal Influence*, Glancoe, 1955.

39 Armstrong, Michael, and Young, Michael, *New Look at Comprehensives*, Fabian Research Series 237, 1964.

40 Floud and Halsey, *op. cit.* (1961), p. 89.

41 Taylor, William, 'Family School and Society', in Craft, Maurice, *et. al.*, *Linking Home and School*, Longmans, 1967, p. 233.

42 In the L.C.C. publication, *London Comprehensive Schools* (1961) we read, 'None of the schools bases its organisation upon the impractical assumption that teaching groups covering the whole range of ability are suitable or desirable', p. 32.

43 Crosland, C. A. R., *The Future of Socialism*, Cape 1963, p. 202.

44 See for just a few examples, Bernstein, Basil, 'Social Class and linguistic Development: A Theory of Social Learning' in Halsey *et. al.*, *op. cit.*, pp. 288–314; Douglas, J. W. B., *The Home and the School*, MacGibbon and Kee, 1964, pp. 60–5 and 159–62; Jackson, Brian, Streaming: *An Education System in Miniature*, Routledge, 1964.

45 *The Primary School*, H.M.S.O. (1931). Appendix III, p. 258.

46 *The Norwood Report*, H.M.S.O. (1943).

47 This was noted in the Crowther Report, *Op. cit.*

48 The distinction between equality of opportunity for equal talent and equality of opportunity to develop equal talent is attributed to Crosland. Cited in Vaizey, John, *Britain in the Sixties: Education for Tomorrow*, Penguin, 1962, p. 16. But see also Tawney, R. H., *Equality*, New York, 1931, p. 123.

49 Himmelweit, H. T., *et. al.*, 'The Views of Adolescents on Some Aspects of the Class Structure', *Brit. Journ. Sociol.* III (1952), pp. 148–72.

50 Jahoda, G., 'Job Attitude and Job Choice among Secondary Modern School Leavers', *Occupational Psychology* (July 1952), pp. 125–40; Wilson, M. D., 'The Vocational Preferences of Secondary Modern School Children', *Brit. Journ. Educ. Psychol.* (June, 1953), pp. 97–113 and November, pp. 163–79.

51 See for example Hargreaves, David H., *Social Relations in a Secondary School*, Routledge, 1967, especially Chapter 4. The existing literature on sociometric relationships in school will be discussed in *Chapter 5*.

2

The Development of Talent

We have seen that discontent with the tripartite organization of secondary education stems not so much from rejection of selection in general as from distaste for the present mode of selection. Advocates of comprehensive education argue that, under the system instigated by the 1944 Act, such selection takes place too early and on the basis of inadequate criteria. For it is now accepted that talent is not a fixed genetic trait, there is no finite 'pool of ability' to be tapped by increasingly sophisticated selection procedures.[1] Talent, rather than being given by birth is, it is now believed, partly produced by school experience. Thus the predictive power of intelligence and aptitude tests reflects nothing more than a self-fulfilling prophecy.[2] Full development of talent is thus prevented by a system under which children learn to limit their achievement to that which is expected of them.

In his 'Argument for Comprehensive Schools', for example, Townsend attacks the assumption of a constant level of ability on which the existing educational structure is said to rest, arguing that 'many of our ideas about the pattern of individual ability are derived unconsciously from the social structure.' We believe that only about one child in five is capable of benefiting from a grammar school education, he says, because at present only one in five does so.[3] Replacement of selection at Eleven Plus by comprehensive education could result in a greatly increased number of children benefiting from a more academic education. The suggestion is, in fact, that '*Comprehensive schools will produce a greater development of talent than tripartite schools.*'

Before we can examine this first hypothesis it is necessary to clarify the concept of talent itself. For the term is, of course, ambiguous. 'Sometimes it refers to an aptitude or ability *in* the person, and sometimes it refers to talented performance *by* the person – i.e., behaviour which goes beyond the ordinary in meeting some criterion of desirability. We shall try to keep our meaning clear by using terms like *ability* or *talent potential* for the first meaning, and *talented performance* for the second.'[4] Usually, in fact, we assume that the two are correlated, for when one seeks to identify talent one hopes to isolate individuals with talent potential who will some time later produce talented performances. Sometimes, as with the selection of children for grammar school, one type of talented performance (success in the Eleven-Plus examination) is taken as a predictor of another type of talented performance (success in G.C.E. examinations or perhaps entry to university). But here an assumption is being made: it is assumed that these discreet *behaviours* or talented performances are linked by a *personality characteristic*, talent potential or ability.

For when we state that individuals who consistently produce talented behaviours 'possess' ability we are making the purely pragmatic assumption that they will go on producing talented performances in those types of activities. 'Anybody may accidentally hit a nail head at a hundred yards with a rifle; only a marksman can do so consistently and reliably'.[5] It is only the marksman to whom we would attribute the *ability* to do so. But this does not mean that ability (or intelligence or any similar concept) actually *exists* in individuals. It is simply a concept which we find useful in describing their conduct, and which enables us to predict with some accuracy the way they will behave in the future. Eysenck makes this point most forcefully in his discussions of intelligence testing.[6]

It is often thought that scientific concepts refer to things which actually exist, and that the scientist's cleverness lies in isolating these really existing things and measuring them. Thus it might be thought that bodies have length, and that the scientist discovers this fact and then proceeds to measure that length. Similarly it might be thought that people have intelligence and that the scientist discovers this fact and then proceeds to measure this intelligence. Thus we would be dealing with scientific laws and concepts which existed in nature independently of man, and which could be discovered by diligent research.

Ability and intelligence, then, like length do not exist in the 'real world', they are man-made aids to understanding and prediction. And therefore in considering how to measure them we are not looking for those measures which would best reflect some real situation, but those which give the greatest reliability in prediction.[7] If a test of an eleven-year-old child's 'intelligence' enables us to predict fairly accurately how he will perform academically four years later when he takes his G.C.E. examination, then it simply does not matter that the test has measured his speed and persistence at solving problems as well as whatever we meant by 'intelligence'.

Yet if by talent we mean both talented performance and a trait or ability consistently to produce talented performances in various spheres, what of the hypothesis that comprehensive schools will produce a greater development of talent than tripartite schools? Obviously the hypothesis implies that the frequency of talented performances and of individuals with the ability to produce such performances will be increased in comprehensive relative to tripartite schools.

Let us look at the first suggestion, that comprehensive education fosters talented performances. This could, of course, refer to any number of different spheres of activity. It may be being argued that comprehensive school children are more likely to win Olympic medals, Academy Awards, Nobel Prizes or Oscars, or merely that they will be more likely to do better than others when they turn their energies to sport, painting, academic work or, say, film-making. On the other hand, the hypothesis may be given an even broader interpretation, it might be being argued, for example, that 'talented' social behaviour is more frequent among the comprehensively educated, they are more dramaturgically aware, more sensitive to others, more skilled at manipulating social situations.

It is, however, more likely that those who hypothesize an increase in talented performances in such schools are referring to something much more specific and limited. They mean that the average standard of academic work in the comprehensive school will be raised and as an index of this they point especially to performance in public examinations. Thus, despite statements by some proponents of comprehensive schools that the success of these schools is not to be judged by their examination results,[8] others insist on comparing success rates in the G.C.E. 'O' and 'A' levels between comprehensive and traditional schools. Pedley, for example, conducted an inquiry into the G.C.E. performance of pupils from twenty comprehensives who had joined these schools in 1954 at the age of eleven. He noted that, despite the fact that many of these schools were 'creamed' by local grammar schools, 14 per cent of the pupils in his sample gained five or more 'O' level passes. This compared with a national figure of about 10 per cent for tripartite schools. This Pedley claims 'bears out a simple thesis: that selection at eleven is premature and inaccurate, and cannot be wholly put right by a makeshift attempt at later transfers; and that if one keeps open the door of full opportunity, many more children will pass through it'.[9]

But, as Robin Davis has pointed out, Pedley's claims were based on the figures up to 1962, before the secondary modern schools had started to enter candidates for G.C.E. on a large scale.[10] When the 1965 results[11] are considered, however, a very different picture emerges. For when the 'O' level results of children in London comprehensives were compared with those of secondary modern school children no important differences emerged. The proportion of the 'O' level candidates succeeding in gaining that qualification was higher in the comprehensive schools in *some* subjects (notably those, like Modern Languages, where their more modern equipment gave the advantage) but lower in others. In other words, even when one defers to the argument that most of the present comprehensives are 'creamed' of their best pupils and can therefore only be validly compared with the secondary moderns, the comprehensives do not appear to be producing better results.

However Davis' analysis can itself be criticized. For the comparative success rates of examination candidates are at least partly a function of the relative quality of those candidates. A high rate of success in one school *might* reflect a very effective school organization and teaching programme. But the same rate of success in another school might merely reflect a very restrictive policy towards examination entrants. One way of achieving high success rates is thorough education of all potential candidates, another way is to select only the best pupils to enter the examinations. If only the very best pupil in the school was entered for G.C.E. that school could be almost certain of getting a 100 per cent success rate!

The supporter of comprehensive schools might therefore reply to Davis that he has not convincingly shown that the comprehensive schools are doing no better than the secondary moderns in public examinations. The comprehensive schools might be entering as many children as possible for G.C.E. in order to maximize the absolute number of G.C.E. results obtained, but in so doing they would be minimizing their chances of gaining relatively higher rates of successful candidates.[12] Further it might be argued that, since those secondary modern schools who enter most pupils for G.C.E. are likely to be those with the largest proportion of middle-class pupils, the comprehensive and secondary modern schools populations are not comparable.

The evidence of examination results is thus inconclusive at present. For in order for valid comparisons between comprehensive and tripartite schools to be made it would be necessary to hold constant I.Q. and social class as well as the examination policies of the schools. Does the working-class comprehensive school pupil of average intelligence have a better chance of obtaining G.C.E. qualifications than the similar child in a secondary modern school? Does the 'bright' child stand as good a chance of success if he attends the comprehensive as if he goes to the grammar? In short, does comprehensive education produce more talented performances in public examinations? At present we simply do not know. There is certainly no basis for the claim that 'the academic argument is all but settled'.[13]

Unfortunately, however, the understandable desire of sociologists and educationalists to answer this question has tended to obscure the more fundamental issues involved in the notion of development of talented performance. For, in their desire to excel in this competition for examination success, comprehensive schools are employing a system of selection through streaming almost comparable to that existing under the tripartite system.[14] Indeed those schools which allow themselves to be judged by the narrow criterion of G.C.E. successes are laying themselves open to the same peril which the Beloe Committee diagnosed in secondary modern schools, that 'if, as on present trends seems likely, (examinations) were to grow in their present form to a point at which they largely dominated the curriculum and teaching, the schools would be in very real danger of finding their freedom restricted and their growth inhibited by Bodies in whose policies they had little or no effective voice'.[15] This would be especially true where some grammar and Public schools remained, for the range and scope of G.C.E. courses would be tailored more for their needs than those of the comprehensives. Thus to the extent that comprehensive schools *are* 'developing' in their pupils the somewhat esoteric skills required for success in formal examinations they are departing from the ideal that 'variety and choice are the keynotes of the educational provision in a comprehensive school'.[16]

Yet there is some hope that a broader sort of development of talented performances may be occurring in comprehensives. For in many of these schools sheer size and modernity make possible access to equipment which is denied to most tripartite school children. In the large modern comprehensives children may learn to turn in good performances in fields ranging from chemical analysis to pottery and housewifery. But if this development is occurring it results not from comprehensive organization *per se* but directly from the superior resources of some comprehensive schools – resources which could theoretically be provided in tripartite schools.[17]

Adequate criteria for the comparative assessment of frequency of talented performances, other than in the limited sphere of formal examinations, have not, then, been developed yet. If 'development of talent' in this sense is occurring in the comprehensive schools no one has demonstrated this. The answer to the more limited question awaits further research, but the answer to this wider question must await the precise definition and measurement of the notion of 'talented performance' as well as methods of differentiating the effects of comprehensive organization itself from the confounding influences of material facilities and teaching techniques.[18]

If the evidence normally cited to support the notion that comprehensive schooling increases the frequency of *talented performances* – evidence of exam successes – is tangential to proof of the hypothesis, so also is that usually cited in support of the idea that such schools foster talent potential or *ability*. For no direct evidence of the effect of comprehensive education on some index of ability, such as I.Q. has ever been presented. Instead the argument has centred upon the reverse side of the coin, the idea that tripartite schooling stunts the growth of ability in the normal child.

The argument proceeds like this. The social class differences in measured ability (operationally defined as I.Q.) have been well documented, a range of up to twenty I.Q. points exists between children of the highest and lowest socio-economic groups.[19] Yet this social class differential in measured ability is not believed by sociologists to be constant. The claim is that as children grow older (in other words as they are increasingly exposed to differential educational experiences through successive stages of selection) the ability gap between the classes widens. For 'the longer children are exposed to an environment unfavourable to the development of those skills which enable their possessors to score highly on conventional tests of ability and attainment, the more their tested ability will deteriorate.'[20] Under a system of selective education, then, the initial social class bias in the distribution of ability is seen to be magnified, those 'favoured' by the system improving their relative ability while those who are 'rejected' by it steadily deteriorate intellectually. In sum, it is widely believed that 'students who enter grammar school tend to increase in their test scores, whereas modern school students often decrease in their scores.'[21]

Now a number of separate studies have provided evidence which is generally taken to demonstrate this effect. Vernon, for example, tested and re-tested a sample of boys at the ages of eleven and fourteen and found that in the second tests those who had entered grammar schools had increased their I.Q. scores relative to those entering secondary modern schools by an average of seven points.[22] Douglas' famous longitudinal study is also often cited as providing data to show that social class differences in I.Q. test performance increase with age and that selective schooling is related to the relative improvement or deterioration in test scores.[23] However, in a recent re-analysis of Douglas' data, Horobin, *et al.*, cast serious doubt on the validity of these conclusions. They point out that there are two alternative explanations of the divergence of test scores over time.

In the first place 'any given test is designed to be attempted by children in a certain age-range and is qualitatively different from any other test designed for children in another age-range'.[24] In other words, while, as was argued above, tests of ability are merely pragmatic indicators of some trait which individuals are assumed to possess in varying degrees, and while we can never apprehend the trait itself but only the so-called 'tests' of it, the tests themselves may vary in kind. Thus whatever is being measured in the standard I.Q. test administered to an eleven year old may differ from whatever is measured by the test the same child is required to take three years later. The divergence in test scores over time might therefore represent differences in the nature of the tests rather than real changes in the relative 'ability' of the two groups.

However, if too pessimistic an interpretation were given to this reservation we would have to admit the impossibility of examining the development of ability over time at all. This would entail rejection of the very assumption with which we began – that certain individuals 'possess' a characteristic that renders them capable of repeatedly performing well in certain activities. And, further, since the tests in question do after all measure the sort of skills that children of the appropriate ages are supposed to have acquired as a result of their education, skills which are anyway relevant in their day-to-day school work, the divergence of test scores is of real importance.

Each 'test at a given age' is thus an assessment of the child which helps to determine his future structural position in the educational system, and ultimately in the larger society. The fact that educational tests have become an unavoidable part of our culture is of far greater importance than their doubtful validity as measuring tools for educational psychologists.[25]

The second alternative explanation of the findings of Douglas and others does, however, lead to much more serious doubt about the validity of their conclusions. For it is well known that, when tests are repeated over time, the scores tend to *regress to the mean*, that is to say, children making low scores tend to improve their scores slightly while those making high scores tend to deteriorate. Now Douglas considered that, since the scores of the middle- and working-class children in his sample were diverging over time, this effect must run counter to the statistical tendency of regression to the mean, and that therefore the results were all the more dramatic. Yet it has been pointed out that, 'Since social classes are not defined or selected by intelligence, *any regression will be to the mean of the social classes separately and not the overall mean.*'[26] Thus analysis of Douglas' tables indicates that what appears to be divergence between the scores of working- and middle-class children over time is in fact no more than statistical regression.

While there are good *a priori* grounds for assuming that social class differentials in measured ability increase with the experience of selective schooling there is, then, as yet no clear evidence that this is the case. Moreover the corollary assumption that comprehensive reorganization will remove this effect has never been tested at all. Indeed there is very little reason to assume that, while comprehensive schools retain any form of selection through streaming, their effects on talent development will differ from those of tripartite schools.[27]

Until adequate longitudinal studies of the test scores and other performances of children in comprehensive and tripartite schools are undertaken on samples large enough to take into account variations in organization between schools, the hypothesis that, *Comprehensive schools will produce a greater development of talent than tripartite schools* must remain largely untested. On the other hand the more limited notion that *Comprehensive schools will provide greater equality of opportunity for those with equal talent* can be tested by synchronic comparisons between schools. In the following chapter, therefore, evidence relevant to this second hypothesis is examined.

NOTES

1 For a recent statement of this view see Faris, R. E. L., 'The Ability Dimension in Human Society', *Amer. Sociol. Rev.,* XXVI (1961), pp. 835–43.

2 For recent overviews of the operation of the self-fulfilling

prophecy of educational selection see Little, Alan, and Westergaard, John, 'The Trend of Class Differentials in Educational Opportunity', *Brit. Journ. Sociol.*, XV (1964), pp. 301–15; Elder, Glen H., 'Life Opportunities and Personality: Some Consequences of Stratified Secondary Education in Great Britain', *Sociology of Education*, XXXVIII(3), (1965), pp. 173–202.

3 Townsend, Peter, 'The Argument for Comprehensive Schools', *Comprehensive Education*, 1 (1965).

4 McClelland, David C., 'Issues in the Identification of Talent', in McClelland, D. C., et al., *Talent and Society*, Van Nostrand, 1958, pp. 1–2.

5 Baldwin, Alfred L., 'The Role of an "Ability" Construct in a Theory of Behaviour' in McClelland, *et al.*, *op. cit.*, p. 200.

6 Eysenck, H. J., *Uses and Abuses of Psychology*, Penguin, 1953, p. 20.

7 c.f. Lundberg, George A., *Foundations of Sociology*, Macmillan, 1939.

8 In the I.L.E.A. publication *London Comprehensive Schools* L.C.C., 4135, 1961, for example, it is stated, 'The danger is that it might be thought that a school is to be judged upon its examination results. . . Examination results are one aspect of its work and it is interesting and important to find out how many boys and girls are being given opportunities for gaining qualifications of one kind or another. It would be quite wrong, however, to attempt to judge a school by such standards and very wrong indeed to compare one school with another in this respect.' (p. 53.)

9 Pedley, Robin, *The Comprehensive School*, Pelican, 1963, pp. 95–8.

10 Davis, Robin, *The Grammar School*, Pelican, 1967, pp. 130–41.

11 From Davis' analysis of the I.L.E.A. results.

12 Indeed there is some evidence that comprehensives are entering more children in an attempt to increase the absolute numbers of qualifications gained. A reanalysis of Pedley's figures, published in *The Observer*, January 1965, has shown that for every 100 children entered for some 'O' levels by all L.E.A.s the fully comprehensive schools entered 121 while the creamed comprehensives entered 172. See Young, Douglas, and Brandis, Walter, 'Two Types of Streaming and their Probable Application in Comprehensive Schools', *Bulletin*, University of London Institute of Education, XI (1967), pp. 13–16.

13 Burgess, Tyrrell, *A Guide to English Schools*, Penguin, 1964.

14 The problems of streaming in comprehensive schools and the

relationship between streaming and the comprehensive ideal will be discussed further in Chapters Three and Seven.

15 *Secondary School Examinations Other than G.C.E.*, The Beloe Report, H.M.S.O. (1960), p. 26.

16 *London Comprehensive Schools*, 1966, I.L.E.A., 1967, p. 17.

17 A review of the wide differences between secondary schools in the provision of these sorts of facilities is provided in the Newsom Report; *Half Our Future*, H.M.S.O., 1963.

18 Apart from the problems involved in defining, operationalizing and measuring the concept of 'talented performance', this research would need to be longitudinal. It would be necessary to compare children's performances in various spheres over the whole of their secondary school lives. Further, in order to control for the effect of size and modernity, comprehensive and tripartite schools of all ages and characteristics would have to be included in the sample. It is therefore hardly surprsing that no such research has so far been undertaken.

19 See for example Neff, W. S., 'Socio-economic Status and Intelligence: a Critical Survey', *Psychological Bulletin* XXXV (1938), pp. 727–57, and Swift, D. F., 'Meritocratic and Social Class Selection at Age Eleven', *Educational Research*, Vol. VIII (1), pp. 65–73 (1965).

20 Horobin, Gordon, Oldman, David, and Bytheway, Bill, 'The Social Differentiation of Ability', *Sociology*, 1 (2) (1967), pp. 113–29, they state this as the hypothesis which is widely accepted among sociologists.

21 Elder, *op. cit.*, p. 186.

22 Cited by Elder, *op. cit.*, p. 186.

23 Douglas, J. W. B., *The Home and The School*, MacGibbon and Kee, 1964. See also The Robbins' Report, H.M.S.O. (1963), especially p. 50.

24 Horobin *et al.*, *op. cit.*, p. 114.

25 *Ibid.*, p. 115.

26 *Ibid.*, p. 120.

27 There is a large literature linking the effects of streaming with changes in measured ability. See for example Jackson, Brian, *Streaming: an educational system in miniature*, Institute of Community Studies, Routledge, 1964. In his Table 19, p. 59, Jackson purports to show how the gaps between the streams with regard to average reading age widen between the ages of 7 and 10. However, when these figures are reworked from a constant base (100) it is clear that, if anything the 'C' stream have improved more than the 'A' stream.

From Table 19, (Jackson)

Chronological Age	Average Reading Age		
	'A' stream	'B' stream	'C' stream
7	8·2 100	6·6 100	5·5 100
8	11·5 140	8·9 135	7·4 133
9	12·7 155	9·8 149	8·1 147
10	13·6 165	11·0 166	9 4 171

Thus, while Jackson's conclusion is widely accepted and it seems, *a priori*, reasonable that streaming affects ability there is, again, little *evidence* that this is the case.

3

Ability and Opportunity

If we cannot, at present, draw any firm conclusions about the extent to which comprehensive schools are *productive* of talent, we can at least examine the extent to which they provide increased equality of opportunity for individuals with equal talent potential or 'ability'. For the most common criticism of the tripartite system is that, while purporting to effect selection on the basis of ability (operationally defined as I.Q.) it does not in fact do so accurately.

Despite the conclusion of Floud, *et al.*, in 1956 that, if measured intelligence was taken as a criterion, then the social class distribution of grammar school places was equitable,[1] Douglas has more recently shown that a problem of social class bias in selection still does exist. The working-class pupil must typically have a slightly higher I.Q. than the middle class one in order to stand the same chance of selection for grammar school, simply because working-class areas tend to have smaller proportions of grammar school places than their I.Q. distributions would justify.[2] It is widely believed that comprehensive reorganization will go some way towards ameliorating this situation, that the extent of 'wastage of talent' or 'uneducated capacity'[3] will be reduced and that, in fact, *'Comprehensive schools will provide greater equality of opportunity for those with equal talent'.*

Now in order to test this and the remaining three hypotheses a sample of pupils in comprehensive and tripartite schools was required. A number of considerations affected the selection of this sample. In the first place, in order for any generalizations to be valid it was necessary to find a comprehensive school which was both typical of the majority of comprehensive schools in England today, and which had been established long enough for the majority of its pupils to have been attending that school for the whole of their secondary education. In addition to these basic criteria it was considered essential that this school be relatively 'uncreamed', drawing almost all the secondary age pupils in the catchment area. For, while the *typical* comprehensive school today *is* creamed of the top levels of ability by neighbouring grammar schools, the theory that we are examining concerns the effects of large scale comprehensive reorganization. It is therefore desirable to simulate as far as possible the conditions which will obtain when (as seems likely) the whole of the public sector of secondary education is reorganized in this way. In this respect, then, the criterion of typicality was abandoned in order to do justice to the ideals of the comprehensivists who rightly claim that where creaming occurs the basic principle of comprehensivization – a common education for all[4] – is lost.

The problem thus became one of locating a well-established relatively uncreamed comprehensive school of more or less average size which also embraced three characteristics typical of English comprehensives: some system of horizontal organization on the basis of ability groupings (streams), some system of vertical organization unrelated to ability (houses), and co-education. '*Cherry Dale*' *Comprehensive* was just such a school.

Cherry Dale school stands on a relatively isolated housing estate somewhere in the inner London area. Built to serve the children from the estate, it is certainly a neighbourhood school,[5] for only 1 or 2 per cent from every year's production of eleven year olds 'go away' to school. The neighbourhood, like most neighbourhoods in urban England, does tend to be socially homogeneous – the majority of the children come from backgrounds which can be described as working-class – however a sufficient proportion of middle-class children attend the school to allow comparisons to be made.[6]

Cherry Dale is in its physical appearance typical of modern comprehensives. The buildings are light and colourful, there are sports facilities, a swimming pool, a 'flat' where girls practice domestic science, and all kinds of facilities for scientific, technical and art education. But it is also typical in its academic organization. The school is organized both into academic streams or teaching groups on the basis of ability and into the mixed ability groupings called houses and house-tutor groups. This organization is more fully discussed in Chapter 5, but it is important at this stage to note that in Cherry Dale, as in most comprehensives, the actual teaching takes place in academic streams. There are, in effect, seven of these teaching groups in each year group, the first two ('A'$_1$ and 'A'$_2$) being 'grammar streams', the next two ('B'$_1$ and 'B'$_2$) covering the upper-middle ability range and the lower streams ('C'$_1$ and 'C'$_2$) being mainly practical in orientation; the final stream ('D') is a remedial group.[7]

Having selected a suitable comprehensive school, the problem of choosing tripartite schools for purposes of comparison was precisely delimited. For, in order to control as many confounding variables as possible, it was necessary to find two schools which closely 'matched' Cherry Dale in relevant respects. *'Gammer Wiggins' Grammar School* and *'South Moleberry' Secondary Modern* were therefore selected as suitable coeducational tripartite schools in similar working-class areas of inner London.[8]

The sample comprised the complete fourth years of these three schools:[9] 320 fourteen- to fifteen-year old boys and girls.[10] Questionnaires[11] were administered to the children in their form groups (or, in the case of Cherry Dale School, their academic streams), in an ordinary classroom during lesson time, and were completed under supervision. In this way the problem of bias from non-response was virtually eliminated, for all the children present returned a questionnaire and it was possible to ensure that practically all of these were completed fully.

The most obvious way of testing the hypothesis on this sample is by analysis of the interaction of social class and measured intelligence as determinants of academic attainment in the three schools. For we know that, under the traditional system of secondary education, the impact of social class on educational attainment is greater than can be explained by the covariation of class and I.Q.[12] In other words, under the tripartite system opportunities for those with equal ability (defined as I.Q.) are not equal and the inequalities are related to social class. If the hypothesis were correct, then we would expect I.Q. to be a greater determinant, and social class a lesser determinant of educational attainment in comprehensive than in tripartite schools.

Now a number of writers have suggested that, where comprehensive schools employ some system of academic streaming (as most of them do) this may not be the case.[13] Thus, on the basis of a study of about eight hundred comprehensive schoolchildren, Holly concluded that 'Streaming by ability within the comprehensive school does not seem ... to result in producing a new elite based on attainment or intelligence quotients: it seems merely to preserve the traditional class basis of educational selection.'[14] Yet the comprehensive enthusiast might well reply that, since no one would maintain that comprehensive schools eliminate class bias in educational attainment completely, the more interesting question is whether such schools are *relatively* more effective in this respect.[15]

Some light can be thrown on this question by examination of the social class and I.Q. composition of the fourth year streams in the three schools considered here.

Social class was determined by responses to the simple question 'What is your father's job?', accompanied by the verbal instruction 'Imagine that you are explaining to a new friend what your father does, try to give as much information as you can'. The information given was in almost all cases sufficient to enable responses to be classified according to occupational prestige.[16] Of course father's occupation as reported by a child is not the best possible measure of social class. A more precise classification could be produced from an *index* including assessments of income, life styles and the education of both parents as well as occupational prestige. But occupational prestige is certainly the best single *indicator*. For its use is based on the reasonable sociological assumption that, since the work role is such a time-consuming one, it is in terms of this that people evaluate one another.[17] Furthermore, owing to the necessity to control several variables simultaneously in the following analysis, the social class variable has simply been dichotomized. And several studies have shown that the most socially significant and meaningful social class classification is a simple non-manual/manual division.[18]

The sample was also dichotomized according to I.Q. scores.[19] Since such scores are artificially created to represent comparable deviations from a norm of 100, those children with scores up to and including 100 were classified as of 'low I.Q.', and those with scores of 101 or more were classified as of 'high I.Q.'. However, as there were no children in the grammar school with scores of 100 or less, in order to assess the relationship between I.Q. and streaming in this school, the pupils were dichotomized at the median point. Thus for this group 'low I.Q.' refers to scores between 101 and 120, while 'high I.Q.' refers to scores of 121 or more.

Table 3.1 shows the relationship between social class, I.Q. and stream for the three schools.

TABLE 3.1

Social Class and I.Q. Composition of Streams in the Three Schools

SCHOOL	STREAM	Middle Class†		Working Class		N = (100%)
		High I.Q.* %	Low I.Q. %	High I.Q.* %	Low I.Q. %	
Grammar	'A'	84	7	7	3	30
	'B'	60	20	20	0	25
	'C'	41	26	22	11	27
	'D'	20	0	47	33	15
Comprehensive	'A's	33	8	59	0	39
	'B's	4	9	56	31	46
	'C's	8	6	29	56	48
	'D'	0	10	10	79	19
Secondary Modern	'A'	31	7	52	12	29
	'B'	11	22	44	22	18
	'C'	0	8	25	67	24

* That is 120+ for grammar school or 100+ for comprehensive and secondary modern schools.
† That is non-manual paternal occupation.

It can be seen from the table that in all three schools *both* social class and I.Q. are related to stream. However our interest is primarily in the extent to which the *relative* importance of social class and I.Q. as determinants of stream differs between the three schools. For this reason *Table 3.2* has been derived from the above figures.

Table 3.2 shows the strength of the relationships between social class and selection for the 'A' stream *when I.Q. is held constant.* Only children with 'high' I.Q.s are considered and the extent to which social class affects the chances of these children to be placed in the top streams of their schools is analysed. Thus, for example, 46 per cent of the middle-class children in the grammar school with 'high' I.Q.s are placed in the 'A' stream, while only 10 per cent of the working-class children in the same ability range achieve this placement: a difference which is statistically significant. In the comprehensive school the relationship between social class and placement in the 'A' stream is still statistically significant for the 'high' I.Q. group, however in the secondary modern school, when I.Q. is controlled in this manner the relationship between stream and social class is reduced to insignificance.[20]

TABLE 3.2

'High' I.Q.s Only: Social Class and 'A' Stream Placement in the Three Schools

SCHOOL	Middle Class % placed in 'A' stream	Working Class % placed in 'A' stream	p = *
Grammar	46	10	.01
Comprehensive	68	35	.01
Secondary Modern	82	52	n.s.

* 'A' stream compared with all other streams in a 2 × 2 chi-squared test of significance.

The results of this comparison, then, give no support to the hypothesis. Indeed they tend to confirm the suspicions of Holly and others that selection on the basis of streaming in the comprehensive school, like selection under the tripartite system tends to underline class differentials in educational opportunity. For in the comprehensive school, as in the grammar school there appears to be a relationship between social class and 'A' stream placement over and above that which can be explained by the well-known correlation between social class and measured I.Q.[21] In other words, at the same ability level the middle-class child stands a greater chance of placement in the 'grammar' streams of a comprehensive school than the working-class child, a situation in one respect not substantially different from that which exists under the tripartite system.

Now it might be objected that to show that a class bias in stream placement exists in the comprehensive school is not necessarily to demonstrate that there are inequalities in educational attainment which relate to social class. For just possibly those children who have been placed in the lower streams of the comprehensive school will achieve the same eventual educational levels as those in the 'A' stream: stream might bear little relationship to level of education reached.

A good index of the extent to which this is the case can be derived by examination of the leaving intentions of the children experiencing the various forms of education. For, if a substantial proportion of those in the lower streams of the comprehensive school intend to stay on at school to follow fifth and sixth form courses, then one could argue that the class bias in streaming has little consequence for actual educational attainment. If, on the other hand, children in the lower streams of the comprehensive school resemble those in the secondary modern in their leaving intentions then clearly streaming has an impact on level of educational attainment and the class bias in streaming is certainly important. In *Table 3.3*, therefore, the leaving intentions of children in the three schools are compared.

TABLE 3.3

Leaving Intentions by School, Comprehensive Stream and Social Class

SCHOOL	SOCIAL CLASS	% leaving in 4th year	% leaving in 5th year	% leaving in 6-8th years	N = (100%)
Grammar	Middle Class	0	10	90	68
	Working Class	0	28	72	29
Comprehensive	Middle Class	0	50	50	16
'A' streams	Working Class	0	87	13	23
Comprehensive	Middle Class	20	60	20	15
'B–D' streams	Working Class	40	56	4	98
Secondary	Middle Class	32	47	21	19
Modern	Working Class	40	52	8	52

It can be seen from the table that streaming within the comprehensive school has a definite impact on leaving intentions, for all of the 'A' stream children intend to stay at least into the fifth form, while 13 per cent of the middle class and 40 per cent of the working-class children in the lower streams intend leaving in the fourth year and therefore have no hope of sitting for G.C.E. examinations. This is, of course, hardly surprising. For the 'A' streams have been following five year courses specifically designed to terminate in G.C.E., and, while many of those in the 'B' and 'C' streams will sit C.S.E. examinations none of those in the 'D' stream are expected to gain any formal qualifications at all. Streaming within a comprehensive school is thus an important determinant of educational attainment and for this reason the class inequalities in stream placement shown in *Tables 3.1* and *3.2* are important.

Another interesting feature of *Table 3.3* is the comparison of the comprehensive 'A' stream and the grammar school children. For the former represent the highest ability group in the comprehensive, children who might well have gone to a grammar school under the tripartite system, yet only 28 per cent of them intend staying into the sixth form. This compares with 85 per cent of grammar school children intending to stay at least one year in the sixth form – a difference which is highly significant ($X^2 = 40 \cdot 2$, $d.f. = 1$, $p = \cdot 001$). This differential holds both for the working-class children ($X^2 = 18 \cdot 09$, $d.f. = 1, p = \cdot 001$), and for the middle class ($X^2 = 14 \cdot 39$, $d.f. = 1, p = \cdot 001$).

This raises in an acute form the question of 'wastage of ability' which was examined in the *Early Leaving Report*. For the table shows not only that 'home background influences the use which a boy or girl will make of a grammar school education'[22] (18 per cent more middle than working-class children staying on into the sixth form), but also that this same effect of home background can be observed in the comprehensive 'A' streams. For half the middle class 'A' stream children in the sample and only 13 per cent of the working class ones intended to stay beyond the fifth. Indeed it seems from these figures that this 'wastage' is even greater in the comprehensive than in the grammar school.

In order to investigate this alarming possibility it is necessary to compare the leaving intentions of those working-class children who are 'able' enough to profit from sixth form courses under the two systems. For this purpose 'able' children were arbitrarily defined as those with an I.Q. score of 111 or more – approximately the average level for grammar school pupils.[23] The number of such children in the secondary modern school and comprehensive 'B' to 'D' streams was, of course, too small to be considered.

TABLE 3.4

Working Class Children with I.Q. scores of 111 or more: Leaving Intentions by Type of Schooling

	Leaving in 5th Year %	Staying into Sixth Form %	N = (100%)
Grammar School	31	69	23
Comprehensive 'A' stream	84	16	19

$(X^2 = 10.98, d.f. = 1, p = .01)$.

The evidence from the three schools, then, far from revealing a greater equality of opportunity for the comprehensive school pupil, shows a persistence of class bias in educational attainment under the comprehensive system. Indeed there is some indication that 'wastage of ability' among bright working-class pupils may be occurring on an even larger scale in Cherry Dale comprehensive school than in Gammer Wiggins grammar school.[24]

For where comprehensive school children are taught in ability groups or streams as nearly all of them are,[25] the 'self-fulfilling prophecy' characteristic of the tripartite system is still very much in evidence. 'Ability' is itself related to social class, but middle-class children get an even larger share of the cake than their ability distribution would justify. The middle-class child is more likely than the working-class child to find himself in the 'grammar' stream at the comprehensive school, even where the two children are similar in ability. And even those working-class children who do succeed in obtaining 'A' stream placement are four times more likely than their middle class counterparts to 'waste' that opportunity by leaving school without a sixth form education. Thus while, as we have seen in Chapter 2, there is little evidence on the question of whether comprehensive reorganisation of secondary education will promote a greater *development* of talent, there is some serious doubt whether it will decrease inequalities of opportunity for those with equal talent.

In short there is little evidence from this study of three schools that comprehensive education as it is practised at the present will modify the characteristic association between social class and educational attainment. Indeed one could argue that it can hardly be expected to do so. For, as C. Arnold Anderson has said, 'In order for schooling to change a status system schooling must be a variable.'[26] In other words, for the relationship between social class and educational success to be destroyed it would not be sufficient to give every child the *same* chance. Working-class children, disadvantaged by their cultural background and inferior physical environs, would need to be given not the same but superior educational opportunities. Yet in the typical comprehensive school the average working-class child starts off with the same handicaps that would have lengthened the odds against his success under the old system. And the outcome of the race appears to be no less predictable.

However, a number of advocates of comprehensive reorganization would argue that, even in the absence of any evidence in support of the first two hypotheses – even if there is no proof of the *'educational'* superiority of the comprehensive system – the *'social'* arguments in favour of such schools are overwhelming and reorganization is therefore desirable on 'social' grounds alone.[27] In the following three chapters evidence relevant to these 'social' arguments is examined.

NOTES

1 Floud, Jean E., Halsey, A. H., and Martin, F. M., *Social Class and Educational Opportunity*, Heinemann, 1956.

2 Douglas, J. W. B., *The Home and the School*, MacGibbon and Kee, 1964.

3 The notions of talent wastage and uneducated capacity are employed in The Crowther Report *15 to 18*, H.M.S.O., London, 1959, and the Robbins Report *Higher Education*, H.M.S.O., London, 1963.

4 'A Comprehensive school is not merely unselective: it is a school which caters for all levels of ability apart from handicapped pupils needing special education. The term is hardly justified unless there are in fact within it sufficient numbers of pupils in all parts of the ability range to call for and justify proper provision for them': *London Comprehensive School 1966*, I.L.E.A., 1967, p. 17, para. 23.

5 The notion that comprehensive schools are neighbourhood schools pervades many of the official publications but is discussed most fully in Pedley, Robin, *The Comprehensive School*, Pelican, 1963, especially Chapter 5.

6 Approximately a quarter of the pupils *in the sample* from Cherry Dale school were middle class and there is no reason to believe that this differs from the proportion for the school as a whole. There is some evidence that L.E.A. areas may become *more* socially homogeneous (see below, Chapter 5), so to this extent it is not unrealistic to examine a comprehensive school in a relatively homogeneous catchment area.

7 Of course the streams were not *actually named* in such an overtly hierarchical way. The picture has also been oversimplified in that the 'D' stream did comprise two small separate groups. But, as these were equal in status and were often grouped together for time-tabling and other purposes (for example they responded to the questionnaire as one group) they will be treated throughout as a single stream.

8 The tripartite schools were chosen from areas more or less similar to that of the comprehensive school with regard to social class composition and general neighbourhood environment. In this way it was hoped to minimize the confounding influence of 'neighbourhood context' on educational attainment, aspirations and attitudes. For the classic discussion of the importance of this variable see Rogoff, Natalie, 'Local Social Structure and Educational Selection' in Halsey, A. H., *et al.* (Eds.): *Education Economy and Society*, Free Press, 1961, pp. 243–4. And, for a study of the importance of neighbourhood context in the case of English comprehensive schools, see Eggleston, S. John, 'How Comprehensive is the Leicestershire Plan?', *New Society*, 23 March (1965).

9 Excluding, of course, those who were absent from school on the day the questionnaire was administered.

10 The fourth year was selected as this was the oldest group which could be studied before the sample became biased by leavers. Any study of the educational and occupational plans and

expectations of such a biased sample would have been highly misleading, c.f. Turner, Ralph, *The Social Context of Ambition*, Chandler, 1964.

11 See Appendix II.

12 For good summaries of this position see Lawton, Denis, *Social Class Language and Education*, Routledge, 1968, Chapter One, and Little, A., and Westergaard, J., *The Trend of Class Differentials in Educational Opportunity*, Brit. Journ. of Sociol. XV, (1964), pp. 301–15.

13 For example Young, Michael, and Armstrong, Michael, 'The Flexible School', *Where*, Supplement 5 (1965), especially p. 4.

14 Holly, D. N., 'Profiting from a Comprehensive School: Class, Sex and Ability', *Brit. Journ. Sociol.*, XVI (4), (1965), p. 157.

15 This point is also made by Giddens, A., and Holloway, S. W. F., 'Profiting from a Comprehensive School: A Critical Comment', *Brit. Journ. Sociol.*, XVI (4), (1965), pp. 351–3.

16 This is the Hall-Jones scale. In those cases where the information *was* insufficient or where the father was dead or had deserted the family (about 3 per cent in all) classification was on the basis of mother's occupation. The open-ended format was used in preference to a pre-coded schedule as it has been shown that the extent of misunderstanding of the latter is greater than the likelihood of coding bias in the former. See Colfax, J. David, and Allen, Irving L., 'Pre-coded versus Open-ended Items and Children's Reports of Father's Occupation', *Sociology of Education*, XL (1) (1967), pp. 96–8.

17 For a fuller discussion of this notion see Chapter 4 below.

18 Blau, Peter M., developed a measure of occupational prestige according to the amount of bias in judgements of respondents from different social class backgrounds, and found that the break between manual and non-manual occupations was the most important predictor of such bias. 'Occupational Bias and Mobility', *Amer. Sociol. Rev.*, XXII (1957), pp. 392–9. Martin, F. M., similarly found that when a matrix was constructed between Hall-Jones categories and subjective social class categories the *most* difference between any transition from one grade to the next on the Hall-Jones scale which appeared on the subjective dimension occurred in the transition from manual to non-manual. See Glass, D. V., (Ed.) *Social Mobility in Britain*, Routledge, 1954, pp. 51–75. A more recent review of the English situation also led to the conclusion that 'The two-class

formulation is much more than an analytical simplification of those who have studied class. It is a simplification which has a profound hold on the perceptions of class found in British society', see Kahan, Michael, *et al.*, 'On the Analytical Division of Social Class', *Brit. Journ. Sociol.*, XVII (2) (1966), p. 124.

19 The scores were obtained from school records.

20 Obviously tables showing class chances of 'A' stream placement for children of relatively low I.Q. or of, say, 'D' stream placement for those of relatively high or low I.Q. can also be calculated from *Table 3.1*. However these have not been presented as the strong correlations between the three variables render the numbers involved in such tabulations too small to be meaningful.

21 I say 'appears to be' because in order to make a categorical statement to this effect it would be necessary to produce partial correlations which would indicate the extent and direction of the relationships between the three variables *over their whole range*. The analysis here presented is necessarily crude because the numbers involved preclude anything but dichotomization.

The lack of a statistically significant relationship between class and stream in the secondary modern school may also be explicable by the small numbers involved. For this reason no attempt at *ex post facto* explanation of this has been attempted.

22 *Early Leaving:* A Report of the Central Advisory Council for Education, H.M.S.O. (1954), p. 19.

23 See Floud, Jean, and Halsey, A. H., 'Social Class, Intelligence Tests, and Selection for Secondary Schools', in Halsey, A. H., *et al.* (Eds.): *Education Economy and Society*, Free Press, 1961, pp. 212–13.

24 This finding conflicts with that of Miller. He found that, in response to the more evaluative question 'Do you want to leave school as soon as possible?', 83 per cent of grammar, 93 per cent of 'comprehensive grammar' ('A' stream), 72 per cent of 'comprehensive modern' (lower streams) and 57 per cent of modern school children answered in the negative. See Miller, T. W. G., *Values in the Comprehensive School*, Oliver and Boyd, 1961.

25 Pedley noted in 1963 that 'Out of 102 comprehensive schools recently questioned on this subject, 88 "stream" the children on entry, 11 during or at the end of the first year. The remaining three do so after two years.' *Op cit.*, p. 88.

26 'A Sceptical Note on Education and Mobility' in Halsey, *et al.*, *op. cit.* (1961), p. 252.

27 For example Townsend, Peter, in his 'The Argument for Comprehensive Schools', *Comprehensive Education*, 1 (1965). Townsend himself concedes that the distinction between 'social' and 'educational' arguments is somewhat spurious, as the 'social' arguments (about occupational placement, social 'mixing' and class ideologies) are really extensions of the 'educational' argument.

4

Thinking about Work

'Men's careers occupy a dominant place in their lives today, and the occupational structure is the foundation of the stratification system of contemporary industrial society. In the absence of hereditary castes or feudal estates, class differences come to rest primarily on occupational positions and the economic advantages and powers associated with them.'[1] Thus, for the child, the transition from school to work is a crucial stage in life, a process by which he reaffirms or denies the rank provisionally assigned to him on account of his father's occupational position.[2] In considering the question 'What job do you want to do when you leave school?', whether put to him by an overbearing aunt or a sociologist waving questionnaires, the child is forced to ponder the much more fundamental question, 'What do you want to *be*?' For it is largely in terms of man's occupational role that society defines him and evaluates him: assessments of occupational status 'seem to catch and concretize the impressions that most people have of the class structure.'[3] That ubiquitous figure the 'Man in the Street' assumes the saliency and consequentiality of the occupational role. For, although he may deny the importance of *his* job for his own self-definition he is quick to assume that others can be summed up in terms of the work they do.[4]

Choice of work role then represents a bid for a specific social status. It is, therefore, hardly surprising that critics of the tripartite system have laid considerable stress upon the way in which segregated secondary education produces a narrowing of children's occupational horizons.[5] A child assigned to the secondary modern school has learned to define himself as society is defining him, he not only performs academically as an average or below average student[6], but expresses the desire to leave school as soon as possible and take up a 'realistically' low status job. The process of selection, evaluation and definition which has pervaded ten or so years of school life thus culminates in a depressingly predictable and realistic job choice.

So, while American studies of the determinants of children's occupational choice have tended to focus on the importance of parental social status[7], neighbourhood[8] and ethnic[9] factors, the vast body of English researchers have been concerned to investigate the relationship between such choice and type of secondary school.[10] The studies of secondary modern school children have shown without exception that the majority of these children are 'realistic' in their choice of job: Mary Wilson found that fewer than 5 per cent of the pupils in her sample chose jobs 'unsuited' to their educational standing[11] and Freeston estimated that only 9 per cent of his sample gave 'impossible' choices.[12] Studies by Carter, the Eppels, Hood, G. Jahoda and Pallister have also shown secondary modern school children to give 'sensible' and 'realistic' responses to questions concerning occupational choice.[13] Modern school children, according to Wilson, modified their aspirations to this realistic level soon after they knew their Eleven-Plus results. The children came to learn the range of options available to them, they had 'clear ideas about employment that was "not our sort of work" – "posh jobs, that are for people who've been to grammar".'[14]

Grammar school children, on the other hand, have been found to be optimistic about their chances of occupational success. Himmelweit, et al., found that, in their sample of lower working-class boys in London grammar schools, no fewer than two thirds expected to rise above the occupational status of their fathers, this compared with only 12 per cent of similar children in secondary modern schools.[15] Liversidge's finding, that there are no differences in occupational ambitions by class background in the grammar school while ambitions are strongly related to class background in the modern school, supports this. The occupational plans of working-class boys who are selected for grammar school education are raised well above those of their fellows who are assigned to the secondary modern.[16]

It is not, however, differential *evaluations* of the various occupations which explains the differences in occupational ambitions of grammar and secondary modern school children. In fact there is evidence that children rank occupations in terms of prestige and desirability much as do adults[17] and, while there must be some subcultural variations in prestige rankings there is no reason to believe that children are *unaware* of the extremes which lie outside their personal range of options. Rather the differences stem from perceived differences in *access* to occupations.[18] With George Homans and Steven Box I have suggested[19] that occupational choice be conceived as a rational process whereby individuals attempt to weigh the rewards which would be gained by entry into the various occupations against their perceived chances of actually getting the jobs in question. Thus differences according to schooling in levels of occupational aspiration may stem less from differences in childrens's perceptions of occupations[20] than from differences in their assessments of their personal chances of entering them.[21] Segregated secondary education, then, produces a narrowing of the range of occupations from which children feel that they can realistically choose.

Before going on to discuss whether or not comprehensive secondary education in any sense improves the average child's definition of his ability, and hence widens the range of jobs from which he feels he can choose, it is necessary to examine a number of the objections which might be made to the approach which I have taken so far. Firstly it might be said that the transition from school to work does not, for the ordinary child, represent a 'choice' at all! He is at the mercy of the forces of demand and supply in the labour market he has no more choice in the matter than any other economic commodity.[22]

Yet, while clearly the range within which an individual chooses is determined by circumstances beyond his control – the occupational structure, his physical constitution, as well as the factors discussed above – there must always remain some choice within that range. The critic might reply that, although there is indeed a choice available, the individual need not necessarily exercise his ability to choose, he may drift into a particular job without deciding to do so. 'If it is a matter of *complete* indifference as to which of several occupations he enters, we cannot analyse the choice he has made between them, but neither could he possibly have made a choice. To the extent to which complete indifference prevails, it can only be the selection process (or fortuitous circumstances) which accounts for workers being in one occupation rather than another.'[23] This is, of course, ultimately an ontological debate: is man 'really' a rational self-determined animal with the power to choose, or a determined element in a mechanistic world?[24]

The approach to occupational choice employed here does not, however, involve an *ontological* conception of man as a rational animal; it is based simply on the *pragmatic assumption* that he is. In other words, if we view man *as if* he were able to weigh alternatives and choose rationally between them then we can make generalizations about, and attempt explanations of, his behaviour. For if, on the other hand, we were to operate with the alternative assumption – that man is irrational – we would be forced to conclude that his behaviour was explicable only in terms of particular sets of idiosyncratic circumstances. Yet this would be to deny the legitimacy of sociological analysis of occupational choice[25] For if sociology is a nomothetic discipline then to state that any phenomenon defies generalization is to state that it lies outside the scope of sociology.[26]

A second objection to the approach taken here might be that it assumes too much knowledge on the part of the child. Children, one might argue, do not have clear conceptions of the nature of jobs[27] or their relationship to status, thus to represent choice of work role as a deliberate bid for specific social status is misleading. But, in the first place, in order for job preferences to be meaningfully analysed as choice behaviours it would not be necessary to assume that children have accurate knowledge of the labour market or the conditions at work. For a child with totally inaccurate knowledge of the kinds of jobs available together with a false idea of his personal ability might well make a choice of jobs which, while foolish to an adult observer, is nonetheless completely rational. A rational decision is merely one taken in reasonable consideration of the available information; such a decision based on inadequate or inaccurate information may subsequently prove to be unfortunate but it is not irrational.

In fact, however, boys' knowledge of jobs and the kind of qualifications required for attaining them, from the evidence of the studies mentioned above and my own data, appears to be rather accurate and realistic. Moreover a number of studies have shown that children are quite aware of the relationship between occupation and societal status as it is understood in the adult culture. Gunn[28] found an emerging awareness of cultural standards of assessment of occupations as children progressed through school and the De Fleurs also observed an understanding of the meaning and status of occupations which increased with age.[29] Liversidge gave his sample of fifth and sixth formers from grammar and secondary modern schools eight occupations to rank and found that their prestige rankings were virtually identical with the Hall-Jones scale which was compiled from the rankings of adults.[30]

Far from being ignorant of the kinds of jobs which exist and their importance in the adult world, then, it seems that children are all too aware of the nature of the stratified society in which they live. As Liversidge puts it 'The general picture that emerges . . . is one of startlingly accurate appraisal of life chances by the children, and a shrewd appreciation of the social and economic implications of their placing within the educational system.'[31] And, in the words of one of the recipients of secondary modern schooling, 'You get a second class education and you get a second class job with it. A pal of mine left school the other week and got a job as a lagger. A lagger. You can't get any lower than a lagger.'[32]

One other possible criticism of my approach deserves examination. This is the argument that statements made by fourth year pupils about their plans and aspirations for work are poor correlates of their actual job attainments. The children may not be able to enter the jobs they have chosen, however realistic these choices may appear, and having obtained their first jobs, they may soon leave them for quite different ones.

In response to this criticism it would be necessary to introduce a conceptual distinction. The term *occupational choice* which has been used ambiguously to cover both statements of preference and the actual process of job entry 'should not be used to designate the total all-inclusive process culminating in the attainment of a particular occupational status by the individual'[33] but should be reserved for the subjective plans made by the individual regarding his entry into the labour force. The concept of *occupational attainment* can then be used to refer to a total process of which 'occupational choice' is but a part. For, 'the job that one acquires is conditioned not only by the preferences and desires of the person for a particular occupational status (the aspect strongly implied by the term "choice") but also by many factors over which the individual essentially has little or no control.'[34]

Now, while the effect of school experience on occupational attainment may be an important and somewhat neglected[35] area of sociological study, it is clear that the relationship between educational experience and occupational choice represents an autonomous field for research. My interest here (and this is usually the interest of the comprehensivists whose theory I am examining) is not in predicting the patterns that children's lives can be expected to take *in fact*, but in the subjective *expectations* they have for the future. I am less concerned with the real (empirical) world of the future than with the perceptual world of the present, for it is only the latter which is real now for the children concerned.

Students of the segregated school system have repeatedly noted that 'in shaping the schoolchild's expectations of the future, the most potent force operating is undoubtedly the experience through which the child passes during his involvement in that part of the educational system to which he has been assigned'.[36] They have described how such schooling, by defining for the child his level of ability, defines for him his level of occupational expectation. Can comprehensive schooling be expected to abolish this situation? Can we expect to find that, if the trend towards comprehensive education continues, as it almost certainly will, '*The occupational horizons of children in comprehensive schools will be widened relative to those of children in tripartite schools?*'

In the first place it is necessary to decide how 'occupational horizons' are to be operationalized and measured. For a number of studies have shown that the form of the question asked has considerable influence upon the kinds of answers obtained. Children respond differentially according to whether they perceive the question to be about their 'real life' plans or about their wildest hopes. Thus Stephenson noted that, when invited into the realm of fantasy most children regardless of class of origin 'chose' high status jobs, while their actual occupational plans remained firmly rooted in reality.[37] Other researchers, on the other hand, have discerned little difference between aspirations and plans, Liversidge noted that his children 'having accepted the role they are to play in life rarely venture out of it even in fantasy.' [38]

Now this disparity could arise from the fact that the simple dichotomy between realistic expectations on the one hand and autistic aims [39] or fantasy aspirations on the other, is insufficient to capture adequately the variation in children's occupational orientations. Between the extremes of actual expectations and the dreams made possible by 'waving a magic wand' there is perhaps the intermediate concept of desires. Children's expectations, desires and wildest dreams may form separate perceptual zones. The closest zone is that of expectations, realistic predictions of what will probably happen next month, next year, or in ten years; then there are 'wants' or desires, things that 'could happen to me with just a little luck'; and finally – on the periphery of the perceptual world – there are fantasies and day dreams. Maybe many children rarely wander voluntarily into the third zone, at least with reference to the world of work, others perhaps live almost permanently within it!

In order to capture as much of this variation in job anticipations as is feasible with a closed schedule questionnaire, I asked four separate questions about occupational choice. [40] The first was designed to capture the idea of *'wanting'* (*'What job do you want to do when you leave school?'*); the second aimed to measure *'expectations'* (*'You have just said what you WANT to do. I would like you to say now what you expect WILL be your first full-time job'*); the third invited speculation into the more distant future, but was again firmly rooted in the zone of expectations (*Try to imagine yourself ten years from now, when you are twenty-four or twenty-five. What job do you think you will be most likely to be doing then?'* [41]); finally there was the fantasy question (*'Suppose for a moment that you could have* ANY JOB AT ALL IN THE WORLD. *What would you choose to be then?'* [42])

In addition to the problem of operationalization there is the equally perplexing problem of measurement. Obviously measurement of the degree of mobility or potential mobility involved in occupational orientations (whether desires, expectations or fantasies) must be comparative rather than absolute. [43] The occupational level to which the child refers must be expressed relative to his starting position as indicated by parental occupational prestige. For it is clear that the meaning of 'I want to be a draughtsman' is very different if this wish is expressed by an unskilled manual worker's son than if the speaker is the son of a successful plastic surgeon. For the one it represents a desire for very considerable upward mobility, while for the other it portends a slide down the social scale.

Responses to all four questions on occupational choice were therefore coded relative to fathers' occupations, and six groups were created. All responses from children of working-class backgrounds mentioning occupations of approximately equal prestige to those of their parents were designated 'working class stable', and the tiny minority of working-class responses in terms of occupations of lower than the parental prestige level were also included in this category. Responses from children of working-class origin who gave occupations of higher prestige than the parental level but which were nonetheless still working-class (that is manual) occupations were coded as 'mobile within the working-class'. The remainder of the working class responses, those mentioning middle-class occupations, were coded as highly mobile working-class'. For the responses of children from middle-class backgrounds there were again three categories: the 'middle-class stable' (occupations of equal to parental prestige given), the 'upwardly mobile middle-class', and the 'downwardly mobile middle class' (including statements of preference for jobs below parental level which were still in the middle class as well as any mention of working class jobs.) It must be emphasised that this is not a categorization of individual children, but of responses to any of the four questions on occupational choice. Any particular child might give responses coded into one, two, or all three of the categories possible for his class background.[44]

Initially the hypothesis that 'The occupational horizons of children in comprehensive schools will be widened relative to those of children in tripartite schools' can be tested by considering the answers to the questions about occupational desires and expectations together. In order to do this an index was constructed from responses to the three questions: this will be referred to as the Index of Aspiration Increment.[45] Responses to the question on fantasy aspirations were not included in the index for, as we shall see later, practically all the respondents gave answers indicating extreme upward mobility.

If we consider only the working-class children, for it is with respect to these that the hypothesis has typically been advanced, the Index of Aspiration Increment can be examined by type of school. Now a quick glance at the results of such analysis might lead to the conclusion that the comprehensive school produces a much higher level of aspiration than the secondary modern – a level more similar to that of the grammar school.

TABLE 4.1

Working Class Children: Index of Aspiration Increment by Type of School

Index of Aspiration Increment	Grammar %	Compre-hensive %	Secondary Modern %	N =
1–2 (highly mobile, aspiring to middle class)	69	48	19	88
3–4 (mobile within the working class)	28	34	55	78
5 (stable and downwardly mobile)	3	18	26	36
N = (100%)	29	121	52	202

$(X^2 = 21\ 72, d.f. = 4, p = \cdot 001)$

Table 4.1 might well be taken as strong support for Hypothesis Three. Yet there are two important variables which remain uncontrolled in this table and, unfortunately for the comprehensive, when these are held constant a very different picture emerges.

The first of these confounding variables is sex. It has been noted by previous writers on the subject of occupational choice that girls cannot be assumed to have the same attitudes as boys about matters concerning the work role.[46] The majority of girls are preparing themselves not for a salient world of work, but for the role of wife. For the average girl expectations, desires and fantasies about the future centre upon marriage and home-making rather than jobs. 'In this society with few exceptions males must eventually choose an occupation.... Consequently there is specific cultural socialization for males which stresses the importance of the world of work. Due to this cultural emphasis, it can be suggested that young males will be more aware and informed in this area than young females.'[47]

It follows from the fact that the work role is less salient for girls than for boys that it is less a basis of social evaluation. If, as I have argued above, 'it is largely in terms of a man's occupational role that society defines him and evaluates him', this is not true for women. A girl's social status is not typically defined by her work role but by that of first her father, and later her husband. Thus when a girl chooses what job she will do when she leaves school she is not making the sort of choice that her brother has to face: she is not choosing what she will *be*, nor making a bid for social status.

Now in Cherry Dale comprehensive school nearly a quarter of the girls, and practically none of the boys, were taking a course known as 'Commercial Training.' They learned typing, shorthand, filing and sometimes book-keeping. In South Moleberry Secondary Modern, however, lack of facilities precluded the provision of such a course. Thus a large proportion of Cherry Dale girls (49 per cent) were able realistically to choose secretarial or clerical occupations, and, since such work is non-manual they were classified as highly mobile. Yet, as we have seen, there is no reason to believe that choice of a lower white collar job by a working-class girl does represent social mobility.[48] This does not, of course, mean that the fact that comprehensive schools are able to prepare girls for the sorts of jobs which may have been denied to them by a secondary modern education is unimportant. If only a few girls are liberated from the inevitability of manual work by the courses they are able to take in comprehensive schools then, for them at least, comprehensive education will have been worthwhile. But the point is that such improvement in girls' job prospects does not necessarily represent social mobility, and even where it does, it stems not from conditions intrinsic to the comprehensive ideal, but from material facilities – facilities which *could* be provided under a segregated system of secondary education.

In order, therefore, to obtain a more accurate picture of the relative amounts of potential social mobility in the three schools it is necessary to repeat the analysis presented in *Table 4.1* for boys alone.

When boys are considered alone, then, the relationship

between Index of Aspiration Increment and type of school is altered considerably. By controlling for sex in this manner the difference between the grammar and the comprehensive school in the proportion of working-class children aspiring to middle-class jobs is doubled (a difference of 21 per cent for boys and girls is increased to one of 42 per cent for boys alone). On the other hand the difference between the comprehensive and secondary modern schools is reduced. For, while there are 29 per cent more working-class children in the comprehensive than in the secondary modern school who aspire to middle-class jobs, when boys only are included this difference drops to only 6 per cent. *Table 4·2*, in sum, gives no support to the

TABLE 4·2
Working Class Boys: Index of Aspiration Increment by Type of School

Index of Aspiration Increment	Grammar %	Compre- hensive %	Secondary Modern %	N =
1–2 (highly mobile, aspiring to middle class)	77	35	29	42
3–4 (mobile within the working class)	18	44	37	40
5 (stable and downwardly mobile)	6	21	34	22
N = (100%)	17	63	24	104

argument that, for working-class boys comprehensive schooling produces an increased level of occupational aspiration. The difference between 'comprehensively' educated boys and those who have been to a secondary modern school is not statistically significant ($X^2 = 0·1$, $d.f. = 1$, $p = $ n.s.) while the difference between boys educated at grammar schools and those who have been to comprehensive schools is highly significant ($X^2 = 9·9$, $d.f. = 1$, $p = ·01$) as is that between boys in the two kinds of tripartite schools ($X^2 = 8·86$, $d.f. = 1$, $p = ·01$).

Yet even *Table 4.2* does not represent accurately the relationship between type of school and Index of Aspiration Increment. For, when a second intervening variable is simultaneously controlled the results are even less encouraging for the comprehensives. In order to give support to the hypothesis that comprehensive schooling has the effect of widening occupational horizons, it would be necessary to show that the 'ordinary' working-class child, who would formerly have gone to a secondary modern school but is now placed in a comprehensive, has higher aspirations than the similar child who did go to a secondary modern. In other words it is necessary to control for academic stream. For the majority of the children in the top academic streams of comprehensive schools are presumably those who would, under the tripartite system, have gone to a grammar school. It is only the lower streams of the comprehensive school which can be realistically compared with the secondary modern. Therefore in *Table 4.3* sex and stream are controlled simultaneously.

TABLE 4.3

Working Class Boys: Index of Aspiration Increment by Type of School. Controlling Comprehensive Streams

Index of Aspiration Increment	Grammar %	Comprehensive stream		Secondary Modern %	N =
		A %	B–D %		
1–2 (highly mobile, aspiring to middle class)	77	58	29	29	42
3–4 (mobile within the working class)	18	42	47	37	40
5 (stable and downwardly mobile)	6	0	24	34	22
N = (100%)	17	12	51	24	104

In view of the firm trend towards comprehensive secondary education the results of *Table 4.3* are decidedly discouraging. For, not only are the lower stream boys in the comprehensive school exactly like the modern school boys with regard to the proportion who aspire to middle-class occupations, but, surprisingly, even the 'A' stream boys are less ambitious than the grammar school boys, although this difference is not statistically significant. Thus when the seemingly clear cut relationship between type of school and Index of Aspiration

Increment is elaborated[49] by controlling for sex and stream, it becomes clear that, contrary to initial impressions, there is no support for the hypothesis under consideration.[50]

We have so far been considering only a composite indicator of occupational choice, the Index of Aspiration Increment. Yet I have argued above that one cannot *assume* that children's desires, expectations and fantasies are synonymous. Therefore in *Table 4.4* responses of the working-class boys to the four items on occupational choice are separately analysed by educational experience.

The trend observed for the Index is also clear for its separate components. If we consider, for example, responses to the question 'What job do you want to do...', the 'A' stream comprehensive school boys have similar levels of aspiration to those in the grammar school while the lower stream comprehensive school boys resemble those in the secondary modern. This is also largely true for expectations. However, when expectations of initial job level are compared with those for ten years hence, an interesting feature can be observed: the grammar school boys have slightly lower immediate expectations than the boys in the top stream of the comprehensive and slightly higher expectations for the more distant future. While the numbers involved are too small to draw more than tentative inferences from this trend, it could be argued that the grammar school boys are more aware of the way in which status is allocated in the adult world; they do not expect to start at the status level which they eventually expect to achieve but see the necessity to 'work up' the career ladder.[51]

Fantasies about occupational choice do not, however, exhibit the differentials which we have observed for the two more realistic perceptual zones. While slightly more working-class boys in the grammar school 'dream' of middle-class jobs than do so in either of the other schools this difference is not statistically significant. For the working-class boys occupational day dreams tended to centre on jobs of uniformly high status and in all groups fantasy aspirations greatly exceeded both desires and expectations.

There were a few exceptions. One boy answered the fantasy question with 'I'm happy just as I am.' Another wanted to be a railway porter like his dad, he expected to achieve this

TABLE 4.4

Working Class Boys: Occupational Desires, Immediate Expectations, Expectations for the Following Ten Years, and Fantasies by Type of School Experience, Controlling for Comprehensive Streams

SCHOOL TYPE	ITEM	Highly mobile Working Class %	Mobile within the Working Class %	Working Class stable %	Don't know %	N = (100%)
Grammar	Occupational desires	47	18	0	35	17
	Immediate expectations	35	40	24	0	17
	Expectations for ten years	65	30	5	0	17
	Job fantasies	94	0	0	6	17
Comprehensive 'A' stream	Occupational desires	42	8	0	50	12
	Immediate expectations	50	50	0	0	12
	Expectations for ten years	50	50	0	0	12
	Job fantasies	84	8	0	8	12
Comprehensive 'B'-'D' streams	Occupational desires	26	43	26	6	51
	Immediate expectations	19	53	25	2	51
	Expectations for ten years	28	42	26	4	51
	Job fantasies	72	6	9	13	51
Secondary Modern	Occupational desires	16	28	28	28	24
	Immediate expectations	24	32	36	8	24
	Expectations for ten years	32	36	28	4	24
	Job fantasies	84	8	0	8	24
						104

59

ambition and considered that in ten years he would still be a railway porter, but, when invited to step into the zone of fantasy, he wrote 'If only I could be a long distance lorry driver.' A tiny minority found the world of fantasy too elusive – even when coaxed they could not depart from reality: 'It's silly, Miss. You *can't* be anything at all.' But the majority of the working-class boys would, if they could somehow change the world, place themselves in prestigeful occupations. At the same time those who were not selected for the educational escalator to middle-class jobs knew that this was not possible. These children knew what was available to them and, whether they were educated in cream-tiled South Moleberry or glass and mosaic Cherry Dale, they shaped not only their expectations but their desires accordingly.

While most children, then, are capable of climbing to the top of a tree to see a more distant field, most of the time they stand on the ground. According to their point of elevation they see only a part of the occupational panorama, and it is within these horizons that they make their choices of jobs. I have been arguing that these horizons are determined by school experience and that for the working-class child of average ability it makes little difference whether he is placed in a secondary modern school or in the lower streams of a comprehensive.

Now one could object that I have not *demonstrated* this. I have only shown that, when the working-class male population of the secondary modern school is compared with that in the lower streams of the comprehensive, no significant differences in occupational choice behaviour appear. To argue from this that any average working-class child would tend to end up making the same occupational choice whichever of the two schools he attended is to entail the ecological fallacy.[52] For it is not legitimate to argue from similar distributions of occupational aspirations in the two *groups* to the statement that the *individuals* in the schools would have had similar aspirations even if they had been to different schools. In order to make the latter inference it is necessary to ascertain that the two populations are indeed comparable, for the findings presented above could be artefacts of the differential intakes of the schools.[53]

In the first place it could be argued that the two populations are not comparable in *ability*. For, since the tripartite and comprehensive systems rarely operate in isolation from one another, the majority of comprehensive schools are 'creamed': the top layer of ability is skimmed off by the grammar schools depriving the comprehensives of the best of their potential intake.[54] Therefore the distribution of ability in the comprehensive schools is depressed and, since ability is obviously a factor affecting job choice, the low level of occupational aspiration among comprehensive school pupils may be attributed to this.

This is a serious consideration. However it was possible to control for the factor of ability in two ways. Firstly Cherry Dale comprehensive school was initially selected partly because it is one of the very few virtually uncreamed comprehensive schools in England and Wales. As was explained in the previous chapter this school is a neighbourhood school in the fullest sense of the expression, it is set on a relatively isolated housing estate and is attended by almost all the children from that estate for the whole of their school lives. For every year's intake (now averaging about two hundred and thirty) only one or two children 'go away' to school. It therefore seems reasonable to assume that the distribution of ability in the school is not distorted by creaming.

However the critic might reply that the pattern of ability in the catchment area of the school might itself, by some freak of demography, be distorted, that there never was any ability on the Cherry Dale estate to be creamed off! Since the argument so far has concerned only working-class boys, it now becomes necessary to demonstrate that the 'ordinary' working-class boy in the B, C or D stream of Cherry Dale is as 'bright' as his counterpart at South Moleberry. In fact the mean I.Q. for lower stream working-class boys at Cherry Dale was 98 while at South Moleberry working-class boys averaged 102, a difference of only four points which is insignificant.

A second intake factor that must be considered is *social class*. For, although social class is in one sense controlled in the analysis, this crude dichotomy according to whether the respondents' fathers are engaged in manual or non-manual occupations may blanket important intra-class differentials. Let us suppose for the sake of argument that most of the working-class boys at the secondary modern school have fathers in skilled manual jobs, while most of those at the comprehensive school have fathers in unskilled manual work. In this case one would, *ceteris paribus*, expect that more of the secondary modern school boys would aspire to middle-class jobs, for the distance to a non-manual prestige level is shorter if the starting point is skilled manual than if it is unskilled manual. The comparison between the two schools could then be seen to be unfair, for what appeared to be the same level of aspiration on the part of the comprehensive school children would in fact represent a greater degree of occupational ambition than that in the modern school. Therefore in *Table 4.5* the two groups are analysed by fathers' occupational prestige levels.

TABLE 4.5

Working Class Boys: School Experience by Father's Occupation

	Skilled manual	Semi-skilled	Unskilled and unemployed	N = (100%)
Comprehensive 'B'–'D' streams %	30	46	24	51
Secondary Modern %	42	33	25	24

$X^2 = 1.46$, 2 *d.f.*, p = n.s. There are no significant differences between the two populations with regard to parental prestige level

It is clear then that the results considered above cannot be attributed to idiosyncracies in the intake of the schools considered. The conclusion is inescapable: comprehensive education has little effect on the occupational choice of a working-class boy of average ability, that choice is substantially the same as it would have been if he had attended a secondary modern school. The results give no support to the hypothesis that the occupational horizons of working-class boys in comprehensive schools are widened in comparison with those of children in tripartite schools.[55]

Yet perhaps I have been interpreting the hypothesis too narrowly. It may be that what people mean when they talk about 'widening occupational horizons' is something more than *level* of occupational aspiration. Perhaps 'widening' should be understood in a qualitative rather than quantitative sense, to refer to occupational attitudes as well as choice of jobs. For, as Carter puts it, 'Well over a third of all secondary modern leavers . . . did not expect much from school and do not expect a great deal from work.'[56] Such children see work only as a means to an end and, even before they actually leave school, they anticipate that they will gain no intrinsic enjoyment from the jobs they will do. They have learned at least one thing from their second-class education, that they are second-class citizens condemned to second-class jobs which offer little but boredom.

Critics of the tripartite system commonly stress the role of early selection in the production of a group of workers who find no meaning of satisfaction in the work they do, who, in Mills' famous words 'sell little pieces of themselves in order to try to buy them back each night with the coin of "fun" '.[57] Usually this 'fun' is something of which the critics disapprove such as involvement in commercialized youth culture[58] or behaviour which is classified as delinquent.[59] But are there any grounds for believing that the abolition of segregated secondary education will lead to a change in this state of affairs?

In 1959 a *Gallup* Survey of a sample of British youth produced firm evidence that orientations towards work are related to school experience.[60] In an attempt to replicate this in part and compare tripartite with comprehensive pupils, I asked my respondents to rank six 'things you might hope to get from a job' in order of importance.[61] In *Table 4.6* their responses are analysed by school type with parental social class controlled.

As far as the tripartite schoolchildren are concerned the results of *Table 4.6* are in very close agreement with those of the *Gallup* Survey. If we look at the third job condition, for example, 'A Good Wage' we see that while about a fifth to a quarter of all the tripartite school pupils pick this feature as *most* important, 62 per cent of the middle-class grammar school children consider it to be relevant (that is, rank it first, second or third) compared with 84 per cent from the same social background in the secondary modern school. For working-class children a similar, though less marked, differential obtains (76 per cent compared with 87 per cent).[62] Just as instrumental orientations towards work are more frequent in the secondary modern than the grammar school so intrinsic attitudes are more characteristic

TABLE 4.6*

Percentage of children who indicate job conditions as most important (ranked first) and as relevant (ranked in first three) by school and social class

	1 Friendly work mates	2 Long holidays	3 A good wage	4 Chances of promotion	5 Use of abilities	6 Plenty of free time	N =
GRAMMAR SCHOOL							
Working Class							
Most important	21	0	21	17	42	0	29
Relevant	58	10	76	65	83	7	
Middle Class							
Most important	18	0	19	22	38	1	68
Relevant	54	15	62	81	74	12	
COMPREHENSIVE 'A' STREAM							
Working Class							
Most important	9	0	30	31	26	4	23
Relevant	57	0	79	83	70	13	
Middle Class							
Most important	12	0	31	25	31	0	16
Relevant	56	12	100	56	75	0	
COMPREHENSIVE 'B'-'D' STREAMS							
Working Class							
Most important	20	0	27	33	20	1	98
Relevant	62	2	100	80	52	4	
Middle Class							
Most important	7	0	33	53	7	0	15
Relevant	53	0	100	80	53	13	
SECONDARY MODERN							
Working Class							
Most important	21	0	27	27	21	2	52
Relevant	67	15	87	77	50	4	
Middle Class							
Most important	16	0	26	26	26	5	19
Relevant	58	12	84	79	58	12	

Base = 320

* After the 1959 *Gallup* Survey

of grammar than secondary modern school children. Half as many working-class pupils in the modern than in the grammar school rank 'Chance to use your abilities' as the most important job condition, and, while 83 per cent of working-class grammar school children rank this as relevant, only half of those in the modern school do so. The rankings of this item by middle-class children also exhibit this trend.

For working-class comprehensive school pupils the degree of instrumentality appears to depend upon stream. Thus while 79 per cent of the working-class 'A' stream children see a good wage as 'relevant' (virtually the same proportion as in the grammar school), *all* of those in the lower streams do so. For middle-class comprehensive school pupils, however, there is a consistently high level of instrumentality regardless of stream, although at this point the numbers involved are too small to draw any firm conclusions. Ranking of the intrinsic condition, 'Chance to use your abilities', is also strongly related to stream in the comprehensive school. For both working-class and middle-class pupils in the 'A' stream the proportion ranking this factor as 'relevant' resembles that in the grammar school while in the lower streams the proportion is similar to that in the secondary modern school.

Table 4.6, then, reveals no evidence to support the view that, with the abolition of segregated secondary education, there will come a change in the way schoolchildren are anticipatorily socialized for the world of work. For job attitudes are at least partly a reflection of jobs. Those children who are perfectly aware that all they have to look forward to in the occupational world is a monotonous low status job, have adjusted to this fact in a most reasonable and realistic way – by psychic abdication from that world. They have learned, even before entering their first jobs, to define work as unimportant, they therefore 'look elsewhere for satisfaction and achievement and see work simply as a source of income.'[63] Meaning and identity, lacking in the occupational role, are sought outside it; yet, tragically as the children become adults each one begins to define the other precisely in terms of that role. The paradox of modern stratified society is that at some time during their education children learn that they have been divided into groups. Those in the largest group come to expect that they will need to perform monotonous operations in order to earn a living. They know that this activity will mean little to them, that their 'central life interests' will lie outside it.[64] But the occupational structure remains the foundation of the stratification system and sooner or later the children grow up to realize that they are all evaluating one another in terms of the work they do.[65]

> At each mile
> each year
> old men with closed faces
> point out the road to children
> with gestures of reinforced concrete.
> *Jacques Prévert.*

There seems, then, to be little hope that comprehensive reorganization will in any way result in a widening of children's occupational horizons. Whatever kind of schools they go to, children soon learn something of the occupational structure and its attendant prestige hierarchy. Yet their choices of jobs and anticipatory orientations towards those jobs are determined not only by the perceived rewards to be gained in the various jobs but by their assessments of their chances of attaining them. These assessments were, as much in Cherry Dale Comprehensive as in Gammer Wiggins Grammar and South Moleberry Secondary schools, largely shaped by other people's definitions of their ability as these were mediated to the children through the school organization.

NOTES

1 Blau, Peter M., and Duncan, Otis Dudley, *The American Occupational Structure*, Wiley, 1967, p. vii.

2 This is not, of course, to deny that subsequent work-life mobility is possible, indeed common. Yet expectations of point of entry into the occupational structure are interesting in themselves. This point will be further elaborated later in the chapter.

3 Reissman, Leonard, *Class in American Society*, Glencoe, Free Press, 1959, p. 141.

4 Contrast this with Miller's view that sociological studies of mobility tend to utilize the index of occupational prestige ratings merely because this is readily available and quantifiable. See Miller, S. M., 'Comparative Social Mobility', *Current*

Sociology, IX (1) (1960), pp. 1–61. I would argue, on the contrary, that occupational prestige rankings are utilized in mobility studies because occupational status is *theoretically* salient: in the real world job is taken as the most important clue to status. See also Watson, W., 'Questionable Assumptions in the Theory of Social Stratification', *Pacific Sociol. Rev.*, XVII (1964), pp. 21–4 for another dissenting view.

5 For an excellent summary discussion of the way in which this happens see Elder, Glen H., Jnr. 'Life Opportunities and Personality: Some Consequences of Stratified Secondary Education in Great Britain,' *Sociology of Education*, XXXVIII (1965), pp. 173–202.

6 The relationship between low self-esteem and academic performance is discussed by Brookover, Wilbur B., Thomas, Shailer, and Paterson, Ann, 'Self-Concept of Ability and School Achievement.' *Sociology of Education*, XXXVII (1964), pp. 271–8.

7 See for examples: Hollingshead, A. B., *Elmtown's Youth*, Wiley, 1949; Galler, Enid H., 'Influence of Social Class on Children's Choices of Occupation,' *Elementary School Journal*, LI (1951), pp. 435–9; Reissman, Leonard, 'Levels of Aspiration and Social Class', *Amer. Sociol. Rev.*, XVIII (1953), pp. 233–42; Youmans, E. Grant, 'Occupational Aspirations of Twelfth Grade Michigan Boys,' *Journ. of Experimental Educ.*, XXIV (1956), pp. 259–71; Sewell, William H., *et al.*, 'Social Status and Educational and Occupational Aspiration,' *Amer. Sociol. Rev.*, XXII (1957), pp. 67–73; Zentner, H., 'Religious Affiliation, Social Class and Achievement Aspiration among Male High School Students,' *Alberta Journ. Educ. Res.*, XI (1965), pp. 233–48.

8 For the most recent of these see: Morland, J. K., 'Educational and Occupational Aspirations of Mill and Town School Children in a Southern Community,' *Social Forces*, XXXIX (1960), pp. 167–72; Sherif, Carolyn W., 'Self-radius and Goals of Youth in Different Urban Areas,' *Southwestern Social Science Quarterly*, XXXXII (1961), pp. 259–70; Sewell, William H., and Orenstein, A. M., 'Community of Residence and Occupational Choice', *Amer. Journ. Sociol.*, LXX (1965), pp. 551–63; Hodgkins, B. J., and Parr, A., 'Educational and Occupational Aspirations Among Rural and Urban Male Adolescents in Alberta', *Alberta Journ. Educ. Res.*, XI (1965), pp. 255–62. And summary discussion is provided by Boyle, R. B., in his 'Community Influence on College Aspirations: An Empirical

Evaluation of Explanatory Factors,' *Rural Sociology*, XXXI (1966), pp. 277–92.

9   See Montague, J. B., and Epps, E. G., 'Attitudes Towards Social Mobility as Revealed by Samples of Negro and White Boys,' *Pacific Sociol. Rev.*, 1 (2) (1958), pp. 81–90. And for two attempts to sort out the effects of race from those of class and culture see Holloway, R. G., and Berreman, J. V., 'The Educational and Occupational Aspirations and Plans of Negro and White Male Elementary School Students,' *loc. cit.*, II (2) (1959), pp. 56–60; and St. John, Nancy Hoyt, 'The Effects of Segregation On the Aspirations of Negro Youth,' *Harvard Educ. Rev.*, XXXVI (3) (1966), pp. 284–94.

10 For an isolated example of an American investigation of the relationships between school experience and occupational choice see Myers, W. E., 'High School Graduates Choose Vocations Unrealistically,' *Occupations*, XXV (1947), pp. 332–3.

11 Wilson, Mary D., 'The Vocational Preferences of Secondary Modern School Children', *Brit. Journ. Educ. Psychol.*, XXIII (2), (1953) p. 97 *et seq.* and (3), p. 163 *et seq.*

12 Freeston, P. M., 'Children's Conceptions of Adult Life' unpublished M.A. thesis University of London, 1945.

13 Carter, Michael, *Into Work*, London, Pelican, 1966, especially Chapter 3; Eppel, E. M. and M., 'Teenage Idols' *New Society*, no. LX, November 21st (1963); Hood, H. B., 'Occupational Preferences of Secondary Modern School Children,' *Educ. Rev.*, IV (1951–2), pp. 55–64, Jahoda, Gustav, 'Social Class Attitudes and Levels of Occupational Aspiration in Secondary Modern School Leavers,' *Brit. Journ. Psychol.*, XXXXIV (1953), pp. 95–107; Pallister, Helen, 'Vocational Preferences of School Leavers in a Scottish Industrial Area,' *loc. cit.*, XXIX (1938), pp. 144–66.

14 Carter, *op. cit.*, p. 109. An excellent description of the way in which hopes and desires are shaped by societal definitions is given by Clements, R. V., *The Choice of Careers by School Children*, Manchester University Press, 1958, see especially p. 15.

15 Himmelweit, Hilda, Halsey, A. H., and Oppenheim, A. N., 'The Views of Adolescents on Some Aspects of the Class Structure,' *Brit. Journ. Sociol.*, III (2) (1952), pp. 148–72.

16 Liversidge, William, 'Life Chances,' *Sociol. Rev.*, X (1962), pp. 17–34. One study contraverts this, see Campbell, J. W., 'The Influence of Socio-Cultural Environment Upon the Educational Progress of Children at Secondary Level', unpublished Ph.D., thesis, London, 1951. Campbell found no difference

between grammar and secondary modern school children in levels of aspiration. This could, however, be a function of the index of occupational aspiration employed. The importance of type of measurement will be discussed below.

17 'Patterns of occupational evaluation found in adult status level subcultures are reflected in the ways children perceive the status structure and function as ascribers of prestige,' Weinstein, Eugene A., 'Weights Assigned by Children to Criteria of Prestige', *Sociometry*, XIX (1956), p. 131.

18 A similar point is made by Caro, F. G., and Philblad, C. T., 'Aspirations and Expectations: A Re-examination of the bases for Social Class Differences in the Occupational Orientations of Male High School Students,' *Sociol. and Soc. Res.*, IL (1965), pp. 465–75.

19 Ford, Julienne, and Box, Steven, 'Sociological Theory and Occupational Choice,' *Sociol. Rev.*, XV (3) (1967), pp. 287–99.

20 Grunes, Willa F., found only a little differentiation by class background in children's perceptions of the characteristics of occupations, see 'Looking at Occupations,' *Journ. of Abnormal and Social Psychol.*, LIV (1957), p. 86.

21 'These youth hold relatively common perception in the aspiration dimension of mobility orientation, but . . . the expectation dimension is more sharply differentiated by their general position in the social system,' Stephenson, Richard M., 'Mobility Orientation and Stratification of One Thousand Ninth Graders,' *Amer. Soc. Rev.*, XXII (1957), pp. 204–12.

22 This would be the line taken from the standpoint of a Marxian theory of alienation. See Marx, Karl, *The Economic and Philosophical Manuscripts of 1844*, International Publishers, New York, 1964, pp. 106–19 where the worker is depicted as a commodity.

23 Blau, P. M., *et al.*, 'Occupational Choice: A Conceptual Framework,' reprinted in Smelser, N. J., and W. T., *Personality and Social Systems*, Wiley, 1963, p. 563.

24 For an interesting review of the place of these competing ontologies in sociological thought see Buckley, Walter, *Sociology and Modern Systems Theory*, Prentice-Hall, N.J., 1967.

25 In maintaining that occupational choice behaviours are rational and hence predictable, I am not, of course, putting forward the view that we can necessarily predict the precise job chosen by any particular child, but merely that the distribution of choices of *types* of occupations falls into explicable patterns. Where children evaluate jobs in terms of mainly instrumental

criteria then their preferences for one rather than another job offering the same extrinsic rewards cannot be predicted without further information, nor are they *necessarily* rational. The children have *chosen* (i.e. rationally decided upon) a category of occupations, but they have merely *picked* (i.e. randomly selected) a particular job within that range.

26 For one of the most comprehensive modern statements of this view see McKinney, John C., 'Methodology, Procedures and Techniques in Sociology,' in Becker, H., and Boskoff, A. (Eds.): *Modern Sociological Theory*, New York, Holt Rinehart & Winston, 1957, pp. 186–235.

27 For an example of this argument see Keil, E. T., *et al.*, 'Youth and Work, Problems and Perspective', *Sociol. Rev.*, XIV (1966), pp. 120, 124–9.

28 Gunn, B., 'Children's Conceptions of Occupational Prestige,' *Personnel and Guidance Journal*, XXXXII (1964), pp. 558–63.

29 De Fleur, Melvin L., and De Fleur, Lois B., 'The Relative Contribution of Television as a Learning Source for Children's Occupational Knowledge,' *Amer. Sociol. Rev.*, XXXII (5) (1967), pp. 777–89.

30 Liversidge, *op. cit.* For an introduction to the Hall-Jones scale see Hall, J. R., and Moser, C. A., 'The Social Grading of Occupations' in Glass, David, (Ed.), *Social Mobility in Britain*, London (1953).

31 *Op cit.*

32 From Downes, David M., *The Delinquent Solution*, London, Routledge, 1966, p. 234.

33 Kuvlesky, William P., and Bealer, Robert C., 'A Clarification of the Concept "Occupational Choice" ', *Rural Sociology*, XXXI (3) (1966), pp. 266–7.

34 *Ibid.*, p. 266. This contrasts with the inclusive usage of the concept as found in, for example, Ginzberg, Eli, *et al.*, Occupational Choice: *An Approach to General Theory*, Columbia University Press, 1951, and Musgrave, P. W., 'Towards a Sociological Theory of Occupational Choice,' *Sociol. Rev.*, XV (1967), pp. 33–46.

35 For a good summary of the literature which *is* available on the actual process of job entry see Carter, *op. cit.*

36 Liversidge, *op. cit.*, p. 33.

37 *Op cit.*, and 'Realism of Vocational Choice: A Critique and an Example,' *Personnel and Guidance Journal*, XXXV (1957), pp. 482–8. Substantially the same point is also made by *Blau, et al.*, *op. cit.* (1963).

38 *Op. cit.*, p. 33.
39 The distinction between 'realistic expectations' and 'autistic aims' comes from Jahoda, *op. cit.*
40 For the actual format see Appendix II.
41 This question was based on 'In what occupation do you think that you will most likely be working ten years from now?' in Middleton, Russell, and Grigg, Charles M., 'Rural-Urban Differences in Aspirations,' *Rural Sociology*, XXIV (1959), p. 305.
42 This form was considered to be more comprehensible to the children than Schwarzweller's 'If you had your choice and you were completely free to choose...,' and more acceptable to the age group than Jahoda's more childish format: 'If you could wave a magic wand....' See Schwarzweller, Harry K., 'Values and Occupational Choice,' *Social Forces*, XXXIX (1960), p. 20, and Jahoda, *op. cit.*
43 Empey, L. T., 'Social Class and Occupational Aspiration: A Comparison of Absolute and Relative Measurement,' *Amer. Sociol. Rev.* (1956), 703–9.
44 In detail the coding of answers to questions 12, 13, 14 and 15 was as follows:

	Occupational Choice Relative to Father's Occupation		
	NON-MOBILE	UP-MOBILE IN SAME CLASS	MOBILE OUT OF CLASS
For working-class background	1 working-class stable	2 mobile within the working class	3 highly mobile working class
For middle-class background	4 middle-class stable	5 upwardly mobile middle class	6 downwardly mobile middle class

This does not, of course, represent a linear scale – no such scale could be constructed unless the two classes of origin were considered separately. Thus, in the case of the working class, degree of mobility increases with code number: 1 2 3. But for the middle class those coded 5 are more successful or potentially successful than those coded 4, but those coded 6 are the least successful of all. The other two logical possibilities, working

71

class downwardly mobile and middle class mobile into the upper class, were not included in the coding. There were none of the latter and those few of the former (less than 2 per cent) were included in Type 1.

For class background classification, in all cases 'working class' refers to Hall-Jones prestige categories 5–7 (that is manual workers) and 'middle class' to categories 1–4 (non-manual workers).

45 The procedure adopted for combining responses to question 12–14 into a single index was as follows:

Class of Origin	Scores on questions 12–14	Index score
Working class	all 3	1
	some 3 and some 2	2
	all 2/ 3, 1 & 2/ 3 and 1	3
	some 2 and some 1	4
	all 1	5
Middle class	all 5	6
	some 5 and some 4	7
	all 4	8
	any 6 recorded at all	9

46 See for example Pallister, *op. cit.*, and Schwarzweller, *op. cit.*

47 De Fleur, Lois B., 'Assessing Occupational Knowledge in Young Children.' *Sociological Inquiry*, XXXVI, 1966, p. 112. Douvan and Adelson suggest in this context that girls' knowledge of the world of jobs is so attenuated that most job choice on their part is stereotyped rather than realistic. They 'found' that 'the bulk of girls' choices (95 per cent) fall into the following four categories: *Personal Aide*: doctor, nurse; *Social Aide*: social worker, teacher, librarian; *White Collar Traditional*: sales, secretary, book-keeper; *Glamour*: fashion designer, model, stewardess.' See Douvan, Elizabeth and Adelson, Joseph, *The Adolescent Experience*, Wiley, 1966, p. 39. However in replicating this study I found that unless coding was extremely lax (does one, for example, code 'punch card operator' as 'White Collar Traditional'?) there were at least three other categories into which girls' job choices tended to fall. Moreover the extent of 'stereotyping' was related to school experience, grammar school girls tending to make less stereotyped choices:

Stereotyping and Realism in Female Job Choice
(Responses to questions 13, 14, 15)

	Grammar School	Comprehensive stream		Secondary Modern	N=
		A	B–D		
Working Class	%	%	%	%	
I Stereotyped (coded as Douvan et al.)	37	57	70	87	58
II Realistic 'grim' (e.g. factory, etc.)	0	21	24	0	25
III Men's professions (e.g. photographer)	9	7	2	6	4
IV Other non-stereotyped (including housewife)	54	14	4	6	11
N = (100%	12	11	47	28	98
Middle Class					
I Stereotyped	35	100	55	67	29
II Realistic 'grim'	0	0	22	17	4
III Men's professions	51	0	11	8	20
IV Other non-stereo	14	0	11	8	7
N — (100%)	35	4	9	12	60

48 It can further be suggested that white blouse occupations are not in any meaningful sense 'middle class' anyway. See Hamilton, R. F., 'The Marginal Middle Class: a Reconsideration', *Amer. Sociol. Rev.*, XXXI (1966), pp. 192–9.

49 On elaboration of a statistical relationship see Lazarsfeld, Paul F., 'Interpretation of Statistical Relationships as a Research Operation', in Lazarsfeld, Paul and Rosenberg, Morris, *The Language of Social Research*, Free Press, 1955, pp. 115–25; Hyman, Herbert H., *Survey Design and Analysis*, Glencoe Free Press, 1955.

50 William Taylor, while expressing the hope that comprehensive education would bring about a 'more flexible set of arrangements, whereby a larger number of choices will be left open for a longer time' did foresee the likelihood that the continuation of grouping within comprehensive schools would produce a situation differing little from that which existed under tripartite. See 'Secondary Reorganisation and the Transition from School to Work' in *Aspects of Education*, No. V (1967), pp. 89–99. A comparison of Grammar, Secondary Modern and Comprehensive school children by Paul Abramson, also revealed far

greater differences between 'A' stream comprehensive school-children and those in the lower streams than between tripartite and comprehensive schools in general: 'Education and Political Socialisation': *A Study of English Secondary Education*, unpublished Ph.D. thesis, University of California (1966).

51 An American finding supports this result for the non-selective schools. See Warner, W. L., and Abbeglin, J., *Occupational Mobility in American Business and Industry*, University of Minnesota Press, 1955, p. 31 *et passim*. Their respondents generally expected to start in the category to which they aspired rather than work up to it. American schools are, of course, comprehensive.

52 On the ecological fallacy see Robinson, W. S., 'Ecological Correlations and the Behaviour of Individuals', *Amer. Sociol. Rev.*, XV (1950), pp. 351–7, and Duncan, Otis D., and Davis, Beverly, 'An Alternative to Ecological Correlation, *loc. cit.*, XVIII (1953), pp. 665–6. The Duncan-Davis procedure could not be used here because the numbers are too small, but the method employed here represents an alternative (to replicating with small subpopulations).

53 My approach to the problem of drawing inferences from the data is based upon the procedure outlined in Blalock, H. M., *Causal Inference in Nonexperimental Research*, University of North Carolina Press, 1964.

54 For an insightful discussion of the way in which such creaming can affect the internal organization of the schools see Young, Douglas, 'Two Types of Streaming and their Probable Application in Comprehensive Schools', *Bulletin*, University of London Institute of Education, N.S. 11 (1967), pp. 13–16.

55 When the responses to the occupational choice questions were analysed by *situs* and *setting* rather than status the results suggested the same conclusion. Horizontally, as well as vertically, the range of occupations cited by grammar school boys was greater than that given by boys in either of the 'non-selective' schools. Unfortunately the number of middle-class boys in South Moleberry School was too small to permit the analysis to be repeated for the middle class. So it was not possible to throw any empirical light upon the common fear of middle-class parents that their children would be occupationally disadvantaged by attendance at a comprehensive school.

56 *Op. cit.*, p. 113.

57 Mills, C. Wright, *White Collar*, Oxford University Press, 1951, p. 237.

58 A number of English sociologists specifically attribute youth

culture involvement to the meaninglessness of work and the education which prepares for it. See for example Abrams, Mark, *The Teenage Consumer*, London Press Exchange Ltd., 1959, and Mays, J. B., 'Teen-Age Culture in Contemporary Britain and Europe', *The Annals*, p. 338, November (1961).

59 Downes argues, for example, that 'the delinquent solution' to the problem of boredom and non-involvement in work is simply a form of fun-seeking which is defined by society as unacceptable. *Op. cit.*

60 A representative quota sample of 15–30 year olds. The results of this survey are presented in Elder, Glen, 'Life Opportunity, etc.', *op cit.*, especially p. 195.

61 The use of rankings made it possible to employ coefficients of concordance for subpopulations in order to determine whether the question was meaningful to the respondents. Coefficients of the order of 0·6 and 0·7 were obtained and so the operationalization was considered to be valid.

62 Chi-squared tests of significance are inappropriate in this case.

63 Cotgrove, Stephen, and Parker, Stan, 'Work and Non-Work', *New Society*, Vol. XXXXI, 11 July (1963), p. 18.

64 Dubin's famous study of the 'central life interests' of industrial workers rests on the basic axiom that 'social experience is inevitably segmented'. The view expressed here also entails this assumption as it appears in the Symbolic Interactionist notion of hierarchies of identities. Each individual is seen as arranging the identities or 'virtual selves' offered by the several roles he plays in order of their importance to him. For many manual workers the identities offered by familial and other non-work roles take precedence over occupational identity. See Dubin, Robert, 'Industrial Workers' Worlds: A Study of the "Central Life Interests" of Industrial Workers', in Rose, Arnold M., *Human Behaviour and Social Processes*, Routledge, 1962, p. 249; McCall, George J., and Simmons, J. L., *Identities and Interactions*, Free Press, 1966, particularly pp. 83–9; Kuhn, Manford H., and McPartland, Thomas S., 'An Empirical Investigation of Self-Attitudes', *Amer. Sociol. Rev.*, XIX (1954), pp. 68–76; Goffman, Erving, 'Role Distance' in his *Encounters*, Bobbs-Merrill, 1961, pp. 132–43.

65 This sort of cultural phenomenon, where all members of a group apply a rule to which they think they are the only exception is discussed in Thomas J. Scheff's brilliant article, 'Towards a Sociological Model of Consensus', *Amer. Sociol. Rev.*, XXXII (1967), pp. 32–46.

5

Making Friends at School

It has often been said that the school can be viewed as a society in miniature, both reflecting and affecting the wider society of which it is a part.[1] Thus one might hypothesize that the peer social organization of the school would tend to incorporate the class stratification of the larger community. And, indeed, studies of American schoolchildren by Hollingshead, Neugarten and others lend support to this view by demonstrating that mutual friendship and popularity scores are related to social background.[2] It has therefore come to be widely believed that the friendship choices of secondary school children are a reflection of their class backgrounds. However the results of two more recent studies suggest that, while class stratification does have an important impact on school peer group formation, this effect operates in a slightly more complex way than had formerly been assumed.

In his study of a number of London grammar schools, Oppenheim observed no clique formation along social class lines; the boys in his sample showed no preference for those from a similar background in their choice of friends.[3] Now, when this finding is taken together with Turner's conclusion that there is more cleavage in friendship preference according to ambition than class background,[4] and interpretation of the disparity between Oppenheim's results and those of the earlier American researchers suggests itself. It seems that the class structure of the world outside the school shapes the structure of informal relations within the school not only through the children's social class of *origin* but also through their class of *aspiration*. For the majority of children, of course, these will be the same, for, as we have seen in the preceeding chapter, only a minority of children aspire to occupations in a different social class from those of their parents. Yet where children *are* anticipating social mobility it is probable that the social status they expect to achieve in adult life is a more important determinant of their interpersonal preferences than their class background. In their patterns of friendship these children trace the imprint of yesterday's class structure more faintly than that of tomorrow. Thus, as Turner says 'this future oriented cleavage may well contain the seeds of class consciousness which will emerge when the students leave school and establish their stable position as adults'.[5] Most of Oppenheim's grammar schoolboys could look forward to a middle-class future. For many, of course, this would merely represent a continuation of the style of life and pattern of acquaintances they had always known. But among those who had come from a different world we would expect to find few who were looking over their shoulders.

Now liberal critics of the tripartite system of secondary education, unperturbed by reports of class-linked friendship patterns in American comprehensive schools, assume that comprehensive reorganization will go some way towards dissolving class cleavages in this country. They claim that tripartite selection leads to patterns of informal association among schoolchildren which not only *reflect* the separatism of class society but also *perpetuate* it. For children are literally segregated at an early age so that they are placed in schools and streams where most of their fellows resemble them fairly closely in class of origin and very closely in class of aspiration. Opportunities for interaction with children from different backgrounds or those who are destined for different occupational statuses are thus severely limited and the hostility (or at least distance) between social classes is thus perpetuated.

For such critics[6] the idea of the comprehensive neighbourhood school 'with its cosy classless ring'[7] is attractive. In these schools it is hoped that class barriers will be broken down, children will mix freely with the 'all sorts' that are supposed to make a world and thus learn the tolerance so essential in their education 'in and for democracy'.[8] Or, as it is expressed in our fourth hypothesis, *'Comprehensive school children will show less tendency to mix only with children of their own social type than will tripartite schoolchildren.'*

Now behind this hypothesis are really two separate ideas.

Firstly there is the notion that the organisation of a comprehensive school does not, like that of the tripartite schools, encourage children to mix mainly with those of similar class origin and class destination because the basic units of the school are more heterogeneous than the class-linked streams of the tripartite school. Then there is the additional suggestion that within their administrative groupings comprehensive school children will show less tendency to prefer those from similar backgrounds and those bound for similar future statuses than do tripartite schoolchildren. In other words it is being hypothesized both that a greater *option* for heterogenous interaction or 'social mixing' is created by comprehensive organization and that children subject to this form of school organization will tend to *take up* this option.

Let us look first at the former idea, that comprehensive schools provide greater opportunities for interaction across class barriers. In the first place it is necessary to draw attention to the fact that the neighbourhood school is not necessarily a heterogenous school, at least as far as class background is concerned. For it has frequently been noted that 'a neighbourhood is itself often a reflection of class, so that neighbourhood schools merely emphasize class divisions rather than break them down'.[9] And there is some evidence of a long-term trend towards increasing homogenization of neighbourhoods rather than social class dispersal.[10] Thus it is by no means certain that a representative sample of all 'social types' would be available in the typical comprehensive school, even if we were to assume the eventual abolition of all private schools.

In the second place the question arises as to whether within these neighbourhood schools the grouping of children for administrative, teaching and other purposes maximizes the opportunities for mixing among the array of 'social types' which *is* present in the school. We have already seen, in Chapter 3, how the academic streaming at Cherry Dale comprehensive school correlates with class background just as does the system of forms or classes common in the typical tripartite school. Within their teaching groups, then, Cherry Dale children are likely to find that a majority of their fellows are similar in *class of origin*. The extent to which these groupings are also homogeneous in *class of aspiration* can be ascertained by examination of *Table 5.1.* In this table working-class boys are analysed by academic stream and the Index of Aspiration Increment as employed in the preceding chapter.

TABLE 5.1
Working Class Boys Only: Index of Aspiration Increment by Stream

| SCHOOL | STREAM | INDEX OF ASPIRATION INCREMENT | | | |
		1–2 Highly mobile	3–4 Mobile in manual class	5 Stable and downward	N = (100%)
Grammar	'A'	100	0	0	1
	'B'	100	0	0	2
	'C'	88	12	0	8
	'D'	50	33	17	6
Comprehensive	'A'1	50 ⎫= 58	50 ⎫= 42	0 ⎫= 0	4 ⎫= 12
	'A'2	63 ⎭	37 ⎭	0 ⎭	8 ⎭
	'B'1	72 ⎫= 62	28 ⎫= 38	0 ⎫= 0	7 ⎫= 21
	'B'2	57 ⎭	43 ⎭	0 ⎭	14 ⎭
	'C'1	14 ⎫= 12	72 ⎫= 76	14 ⎫= 12	7 ⎫= 17
	'C'2	10 ⎭	80 ⎭	10 ⎭	10 ⎭
	'D'	0	23	77	13
Secondary Modern	'A'	63	37	0	8
	'B'	50	50	0	4
	'C'	0	33	67	12

Yet, in order to examine the hypothesis that the internal organization of the comprehensive school creates more opportunities for social mixing than the tripartite school, it is not sufficient to demonstrate homogeneity of teaching groups. For in Cherry Dale school, as in many other comprehensives, there is a deliberate attempt to undermine the influence of academic stratification by the introduction of a system of 'vertical' subdivisions or houses.[11]

On entering the school each child is assigned to one of the four houses and throughout his school life various activities are organized through the house system in order to increase the salience of house membership for the individual children. Thus sports competitions take place between houses and members of the same house can, for example, dine together in their house room. This vertical organization is elaborated by a system of horizontal divisions based on year groups, so that within each year group children are assigned to tutor groups on the basis of their houses not their ability. In the fourth year there are eight house tutor groups (two for each house) each with a tutor who goes 'up' each year with his tutees and is therefore expected to come to know them all intimately.

Officially the house tutor groups rather than the academic streams are regarded as the basic administrative units and it is in these groups that children meet for registration each morning and afternoon. The aim is to replace the form or class of the traditional school by a mixed ability group which moves up the school together and is expected to become a cohesive unit. Thus, while children spend the majority of their time at school in their socially homogeneous academic streams, one might argue that some opportunity for social mixing is presented by the organization of houses and house tutor groups.

However it is one thing to claim that children have some opportunity for heterogeneous social interaction in Cherry Dale school and quite another to suggest that they will take up this option. In order to find out whether traditional lines of stratification are indeed undermined by the house system, we need to know whether academic streams or house tutor groups have the greatest impact on friendship formation in the school. In an attempt to determine this, all the children were asked to imagine that they must choose one friend from all the people they knew, one 'real friend' in whom they felt they could confide and with whom, for example, they could envisage undertaking a long journey.[12] Keeping this person in mind they were then asked to indicate whether he or she was in the same school, and, if so, in which academic stream. Cherry Dale children were then additionally required to indicate whether friends chosen from within the school were in the same house or a different house from themselves. The results are presented in *Tables 5.2 and 5.3.*

It is clear from *Table 5.2* that children in all streams of all the schools are more likely to choose their 'one real friend' from their own form or stream or its equivalent than any other in the same school. In fact, when we consider only those children choosing an individual in their own school (64 per cent of the total), we find that in all schools more than two thirds choose someone from their own (or an equivalent) stream; in the

TABLE 5.2

All Children: Choice of 'One Real Friend' by Stream of Choosers and Chosen

Characteristics of Choosers		Characteristics of Chosen					
SCHOOL	STREAM	Same or equivalent stream %	Higher stream* %	Lower stream† %	Different school %	Left school %	N = (100%)
Grammar	'A'	40	17	3	33	7	30
	'B'	32	12	12	28	16	25
	'C'	37	11	7	22	22	27
	'D'	33	7	13	7	40	15
Comprehensive	'A'1 & 'A'2	57	15	5	8	15	39
	'B'1 & 'B'2	39	4	13	26	17	46
	'C'1 & 'C'2	44	10	2	15	29	48
	'D'	53	26	5	5	10	19
Secondary Modern	'A'	62	7	5	14	10	29
	'B'	33	11	11	28	17	18
	'C'	46	4	17	12	21	24
Total sample		41	11	8	18	18	320

* This includes those in a higher academic stream in the same year group *and* those higher up the school in the fifth and sixth forms.

† This includes those in a lower academic stream in the same year group plus children in the lower school (that is first to third forms).

grammar school 67 per cent do so, in the comprehensive 72 per cent and in the secondary modern 73 per cent, and these proportions are similar in all streams. This means that, of the children choosing their friends from their own school, the proportion choosing them from their own or equivalent streams is always more than twice as large as one would have expected by chance.[13]

Table 5.3, on the other hand, indicates that among the Cherry Dale children confining their choices to other Cherry Dale children (65 per cent) there is no preference for friends in

TABLE 5.3

Cherry Dale Comprehensive Pupils Only: Choice of 'One Real Friend' by Stream of Chooser and Relative House of Chosen

Stream of chooser	House of chosen relative to chooser		
	same %	different %	N = (100%)
'A'	23	77	30
'B'	27	73	26
'C'	30	70	27
'D'	25	75	16
All	26	74	99

the same *house*. Since the numerical strength of the four houses in the fourth year is almost exactly equal then, purely by chance, we would expect one choice in four to be for an individual in the chooser's own house. And the percentages in the table never deviate by more than 5 per cent from this chance pattern, indicating that the relationship of friendship choice to house is no more than random.

Tables 5.2 and 5.3, then, offer little comfort for those who have put their faith in comprehensive reorganization as a means of destroying class barriers in interpersonal relations. For while one might argue that 'vertical' organization of the school into houses provides some opportunity for inter-class interaction, there is no evidence to show that this makes any difference to the actual processes of friendship choice within the comprehensive school. For, in contrast to Pape's finding for a sample of comprehensive school girls that 'they are just as likely to be found mixing with other members of their house who are in different forms',[14] Cherry Dale children are more likely to choose their 'real friends' from their own class-homogeneous academic streams than their socially mixed houses.

Indeed I found little evidence that the houses meant much at all to the children and it was difficult to avoid the conclusion that house tutor groups were no more than nominal administrative aggregates rather than real social groups. For the children were frequently heard to refer to 'our form' (meaning academic stream not house tutor group) and, although I asked them to write their house tutor groups at the top of their completed questionnaires, most of them either added their academic stream number or gave only the latter. In fact a number of boys and girls claimed that they found it difficult to answer the question in which they were required to indicate the relative house of their chosen friend, as they did not *know* which houses their best friends were in![15]

We have seen that the 'real' social units of the schools, whether comprehensive or tripartite, are the academic streams or forms, for not only do these groups spend a considerable amount of time together *as* groups, but also their members show a preference for each other in their informal associations.[16] We have also seen that these groups tend towards social homogeneity in terms of both class background and the future aspirations of their members. Yet this is obviously only a *tendency*, for while a majority of the children within one stream are usually socially similar the correlation is not perfect. In Cherry Dale school for example there are more middle-class children in the 'A' stream than in all the other streams put together, class background and stream are very strongly related. But, despite this fact, middle-class children make up less than one half of the total 'A' streamers, while in the 'B' and 'C' streams about one child in every seven is middle class.[17] In other words, in spite of the strong class bias in streaming, the opportunity for children to mix with others from different class backgrounds within their streams, while greatly restricted, is not negligible. A similar case can be argued with regard to class of aspiration, although here (as can be ascertained from the number of empty cells in *Table 5.1*) homogeneity is much more closely approximated.

There are therefore two more ways in which the fourth hypothesis can be examined. For the extent to which friendship preference *within* academic streams shows ingroup preference in respect of firstly social class of origin, and secondly social class of aspiration remains empirically problematic. It is just possible that some difference between the comprehensive and tripartite schools might show itself here, that comprehensive pupils might turn out to be less 'class conscious' on these criteria than tripartite school children.

In order to examine this possibility the children were asked:

Suppose you wanted to pick some people to be your *close friends* – people you would enjoy doing things with and like to have as close friends for a *long time*. Which three people *who are in this classroom right now* would you pick? [18]

This, unlike the question reported above, is directed towards friendship *preference* rather than friendship *choice*. For the children, who were responding in the company only of the rest of their academic streams,[19] would not necessarily normally choose their friends from within that universe, in fact we know from *Table 5.2* that probably only about forty per cent would do so. Thus 'there is an important possibility that the individual may be forced to choose people he would not spontaneously select, with the result that the choices are arbitrary if not erroneous in character.... If, however, friendship is a relative matter, there is no reason why a subject should not be able to make choices as far down a continuum as desired. When we ask for hypothetical choices rather than existing friendships the problem is less severe. We need only assume that the students know others in the class well enough to be able to make some guesses as to who are most nearly the kinds of persons they would like to have as friends.'[20]

Responses to this question can be analysed by the use of the traditional sociometric methods as developed by Moreno.[21] The pattern of friendship preferences within each academic stream is described by a *sociogram*, a chart in which interpersonal preferences are represented by lines between individuals. Broken lines are used to represent unreciprocated choices, with arrows to denote the direction of choice, while solid lines represent mutual choices. The individuals themselves are graphically presented so that their sex and social class of origin are immediately identifiable, and in addition each is numbered to facilitate identification of particular individuals. Thus the sociometric structure of each stream is described in the following charts.

The most cursory inspection of any of the fourteen charts is sufficient to reveal immediately that responses to the request to name hypothetical friends are not random but do fall into patterns.[22] In fact in most streams a number of separate groups or cliques of hypothetical friends are identifiable, the most tightly knit cliques being those linked by the greatest proportion of unbroken lines.

If we look first at the Gammer Wiggins children we can see that, in the 'A' stream depicted in *Chart I*, there are four small cliques of four or five individuals who offer each other reciprocated choices, plus a number of couples and isolated individuals. These smaller units are connected together by a number of broken lines representing unreciprocated choices, but the pattern of the latter tends to define not one group but two constellations between which there are relatively few connections. This differentiation is clearly along lines of sex, for, with the exception of the three boys numbered 14, 18 and 28, all the boys offer the majority of their choices to other boys and none of the girls makes a single choice of a boy. This differentiation between boys and girls is again observable in the 'B' stream as shown in *Chart II*, for boys and girls are here connected only by the mutual choice of girl number 22 and boy number 2 (the isolated girl numbered 21 also choosing 2). In the 'C' stream the sociometric structure is less clearly defined, for *Chart III* shows a large proportion of unreciprocated choices, but, despite the apparent integration of boys number 4 and 22 into the female constellation, a split between boys and girls can still be observed. And this pattern is again repeated in *Chart IV* from which it is clear that, while girl number 5 represents an important link between the two sexes, boys and girls are more likely to choose friends of the same sex.

Yet, if it is clear simply from inspection of the charts that sex is a relevant variable in the grammar school pupils' choices of hypothetical friends among their form-mates, the same can hardly be said for class background. In the 'A' stream there are

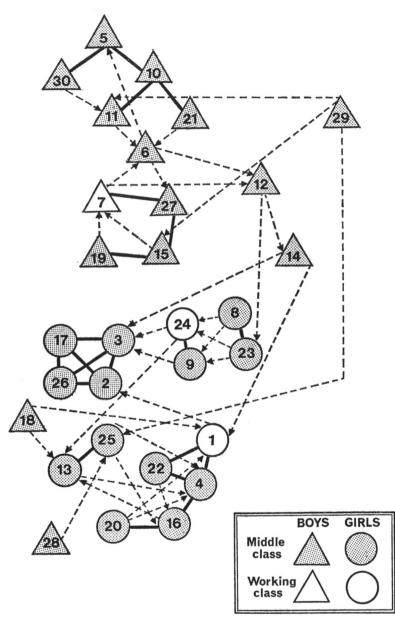

Chart One Gammer Wiggins Grammar School: Stream A

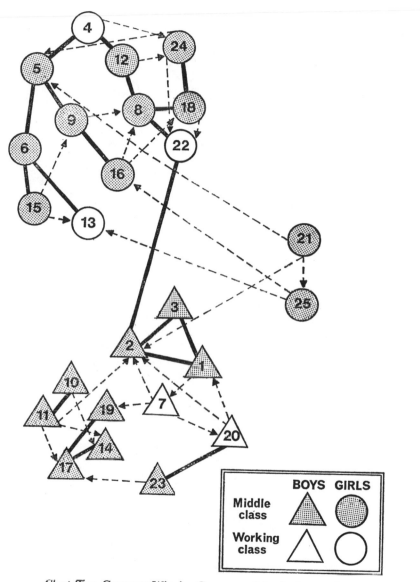

Chart Two Gammer Wiggins Grammar School: Stream B

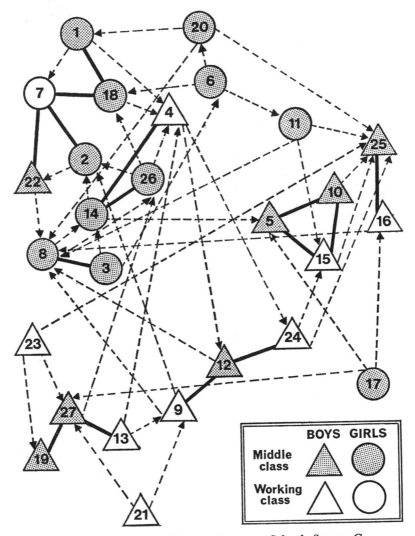

Chart Three Gammer Wiggins Grammar School: Stream C

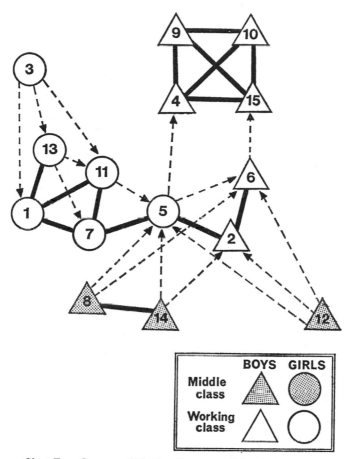

Chart Four Gammer Wiggins Grammar School: Stream D

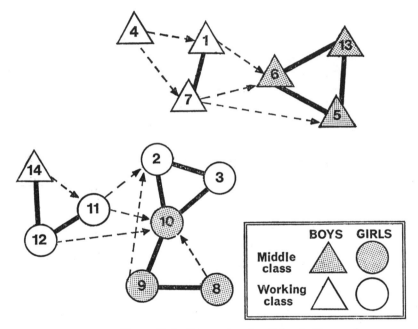

Chart Five Cherry Dale Comprehensive School: Stream A1

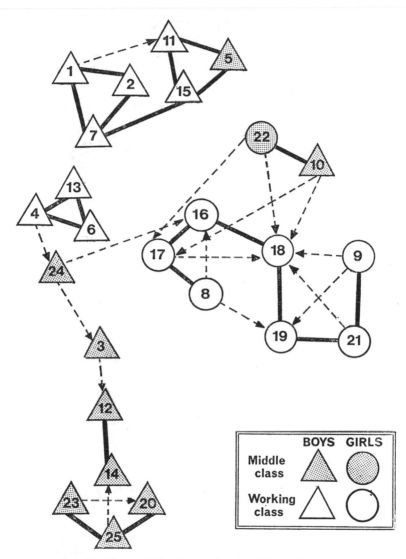

Chart Six Cherry Dale Comprehensive School: Stream A2

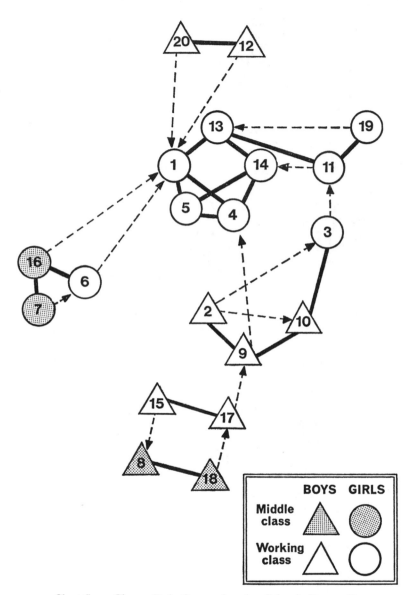

Chart Seven Cherry Dale Comprehensive School: Stream B1

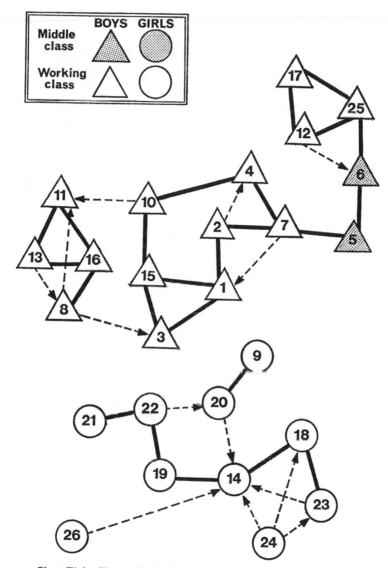

Chart Eight Cherry Dale Comprehensive School: Stream B2

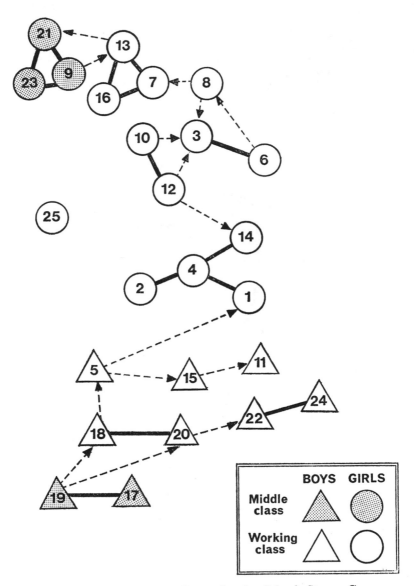

Chart Nine Cherry Dale Comprehensive School: Stream C1

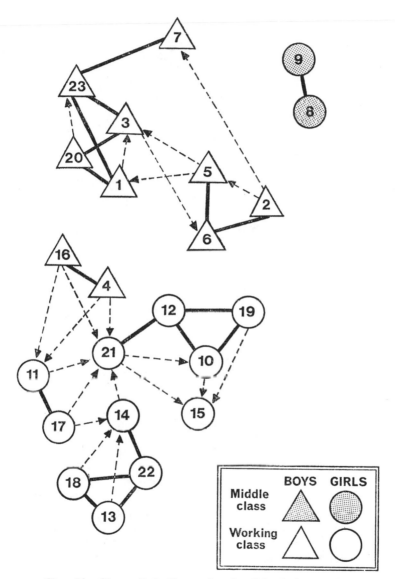

Chart Ten Cherry Dale Comprehensive School: Stream C2

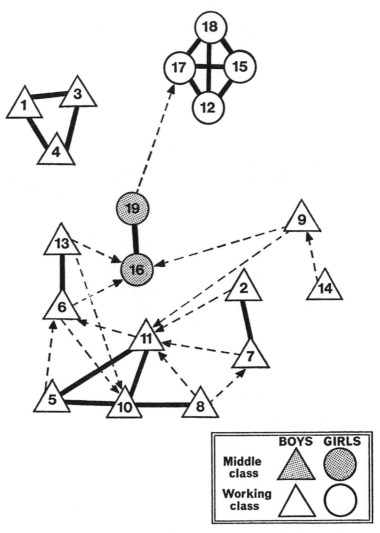

Chart Eleven Cherry Dale Comprehensive School: Stream D

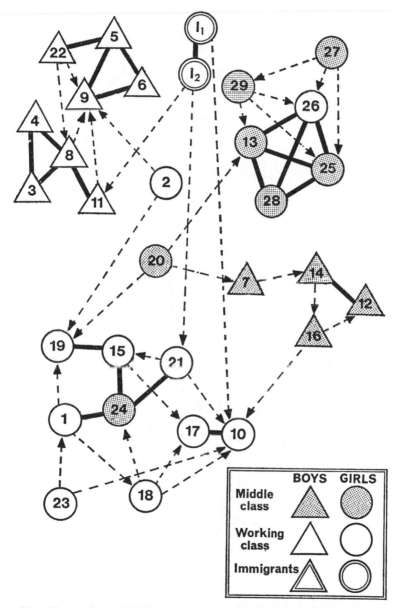

Chart Twelve South Moleberry Secondary Modern School: Stream A

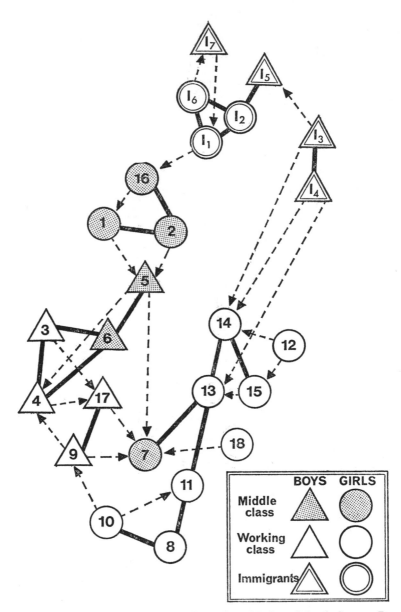

Chart Thirteen South Moleberry Secondary Modern School: Stream B

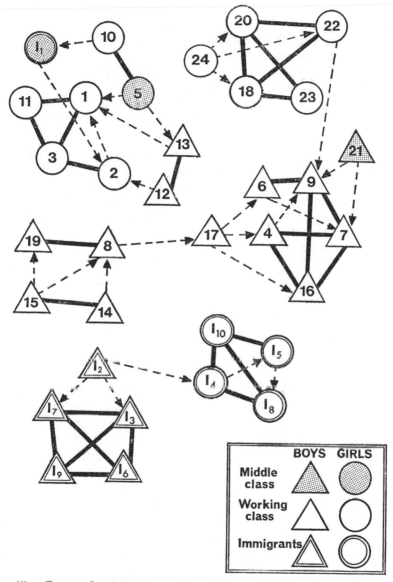

Chart Fourteen South Moleberry Secondary Modern School: Stream C

only three working-class children and they all appear to be completely integrated into the class, for each receives at least as many choices as he or she gives and has at least one reciprocated preference for a middle-class child. In the 'B' and 'C' streams, where the proportion of working-class children is greater, they still seem to be perfectly accepted by their middle-class fellows. However in the 'D' stream, where the numerical strength of the two social classes is reversed, the three middle-class boys do appear to be isolated in that, while they offer choices to working-class children, they are not chosen by them. To sum up these initial impressions of the sociometric structure of the four grammar school streams, then, it appears that, while sex is always a relevant criterion of friendship choice, class background assumes importance only in the 'D' stream. Before analysing the significance of these facts let us look briefly at the patterns of choice in the comprehensive and secondary modern schools.

In the two 'A' streams at Cherry Dale school, depicted in *Charts V* and *VI*, the sex pattern apparent at Gammer Wiggins is still evident, but there appears to be an important difference with regard to social class background, for the middle-class children seem to be forming clusters. In stream 'A1' the three middle class boys (6, 13 and 5) form a clear clique and the three middle class girls (8, 9 and 10) are also closely linked together although one of these (number 10) also reciprocates choice with two working-class girls. Similarly in *Chart VI* we see a tendency for the middle-class boys to confine their choices to each other, only one of them (number 5) being integrated into a group of working-class boys. The one middle-class girl in stream 'A2' reciprocates a choice with a middle-class boy (girl 22 and boy 10). *Charts VII* and *VIII* reveal a similar tendency for the two 'B' streams, for the few middle-class children in these streams, although making some choices of working-class children, always have one reciprocated choice of a middle-class friend of the same sex. This tendency is also observable in the three remaining streams as shown in *Charts IX, X and XI*. Indeed in *Chart X* we see that in stream 'C2' the only two middle-class girls (numbers 8 and 9) are completely isolated from the rest of the group, they neither choose, nor are they chosen by, any working class boys or girls. Preliminary inspection of hypothetical friendship choices in the comprehensive school streams then suggests that, in contrast to the grammar school, social class background plays an important part.

The final three charts depict the situation in South Moleberry School. Here, however, the analysis is somewhat complicated by another factor. There were, at South Moleberry School a number of first generation immigrants, mainly from the West Indies and Pakistan. These were not included in the main sample as most of them had not been educated solely in English secondary schools and it was also felt that educational progress, job choice and views of social class would all be affected both by their untypical socialization and by the racial discrimination which they may have both anticipated and experienced. Naturally, however, these immigrants were included in the classes at the time of the administration of the questionnaire and therefore they formed part of the universe from which the other children could choose their hypothetical friends. It was therefore considered desirable that, if a picture of the structure of a 'real' group such as the school class were to be drawn, all the available 'real' members should be included in the sociometric analysis. The immigrants are distinguishable by the prefix 'I' before their code numbers. Thus, parenthetically, some information about race relations in a secondary modern school can be gained from *Charts XII–XIV*.[13]

In these three charts it is again clear on inspection that both sex and social class of origin are important criteria of friend selection. In the 'A' stream, for example, as *Chart XII* shows, there is a clique of predominantly middle-class girls, although number 26, a working-class girl is accepted into this group. Similarly the working-class girls form one clique which nonetheless includes one middle-class girl, number 24. No working-class children choose the middle-class boys although one of the latter offers an unreciprocated choice to a working-class boy (16 choosing 10). *Chart XIII* again reveals this pattern, although a middle-class girl (number 7), one of the most popular children in the form, links both social classes and both sexes. In the 'C' stream, *Chart XIV*, there are only two middle-class pupils. The boy is completely isolated, offering choices to working class boys and receiving none in return, the girl, however is linked by mutual choice to a working-class girl although this pair

(5 and 10) is not really integrated into the main clique of girls.

Cursory inspection of sociograms for each stream of each school, then, leads to the tentative conclusion that, apart from the unstartling relationship between friendship choices and sex, a striking feature of these sociometric structures is the way in which they relate to class background. Children, in all streams except the first three in the grammar school, seem to be biased in favour of their own social class background in their choice of hypothetical friends from among their form-mates. Yet clearly some more 'objective' index of this tendency is required in order to determine the extent of this bias. For what may appear, from a brief glance at a sociogram, to be a clear trend may turn out to be a pattern which could well have occurred by chance.

In order to obtain this objective comparison the *Index of Ingroup Preference* as developed by Proctor and Loomis was employed. This gives a way of calculating, for any ingroup the ratio of choices for members of that ingroup to choices for the outgroup, taking into account the total number of choices given and the relative size of the two groups.[24] Thus for example, if we consider the working-class children in one stream as an ingroup, we can compare the proportion of their choices for that group and for the outgroup (that is the middle-class children in the same stream) with the proportions which would have been expected purely by chance on the basis of the relative numerical strength of the two groups. The analysis can then be repeated with the middle class considered as the ingroup. The Index of Ingroup Preference (or I.P.) is so calculated that where preference for the two groups is equal – that is where the factor concerned (social class in this case) bears only a chance relationship to choices – then I.P. is equal to unity. On the other hand an I.P. of greater than one indicates ingroup preference (the actual extent of that preference obviously relating to the value of I.P.), while an I.P. of less than one indicates preference for the outgroup. At the extreme total preference for the ingroup would give an I.P. value of infinity while total preference for the outgroup would give an I.P. value of zero. In *Table 5.4* I.P.s for both working-class and middle-class children in each stream are given.

Table 5.4, then, gives support to the initial interpretations of

TABLE 5.4

All Children: Index of Ingroup Preference for Social Class of 'Origin by School and Stream

SCHOOL	STREAM	Index of Ingroup Preference		Numbers in stream	
		For Middle Class	For Working Class	Middle Class	Working Class
Grammar	'A'	0·29	0	27	3
	'B'	0·68	0·45	20	5
	'C'	1·38	0·56	18	9
	'D'	1·71	∞	3	12
Comprehensive	'A'1	5·12	1·42	6	8
	'A'2	2·6	8·1	10	15
	'B'1	4·3	4·9	4	16
	'B'2	24·0	2·3	2	24
	'C'1	13·3	7·9	5	20
	'C'2	∞	∞	2	21
	'D'	34·0	1·6	2	17
Secondary Modern*	'A'	3·06	3·02	11	18
	'B'	5·4	2·72	6	12
	'C'	0	5·1	2	22

* The immigrants are excluded from the calculation.

the sociograms, for (apart from the two middle-class children in the 'C' stream at South Moleberry who do not choose one another) the only I.P.s with a value of less than unity are to be found in the top three streams of the grammar school, although the middle class in the 'C' stream do show a slight tendency to ingroup preference. In all other cases children show a tendency to choose their hypothetical friends from those of similar class background. Indeed some of the I.P. values are really quite high (reaching infinity in three cases where, however the numbers of the minority are too small to give any importance to this value), thus indicating quite a strong degree of 'consciousness of kind' in friendship choice.

The evidence from this sample then suggests that if any type of schooling diminishes the likelihood of class bias in informal social relations within the classroom this is not the comprehensive but the grammar school. Earlier, it was suggested that this lack of class bias among grammar school pupils might be due to the fact that, where class of origin and class of aspiration differ, it is the latter which is of greater importance in the determination of friendship choices. *Ex post facto* one might also suggest that working-class children in the 'D' stream of the grammar school differ from those in the higher streams, both in that they are here in a majority rather than a minority and in that they, unlike their more successful fellows, are not unequivocally destined for the middle class. Thus, whereas in the other grammar streams the fact of positive selection is sufficient to dull the effects of class of origin on interpersonal behaviour, among 'D' stream grammar school children class background again assumes importance.[25]

It would be desirable to test this suggestion, and simultaneously exhaust the possible interpretations of the fourth hypothesis, by repeating the analysis of ingroup preference using class of aspiration instead of class of origin as a criterion. However, as class of aspiration (as measured by the Index of Aspiration Increment) can, for reasons explained in the preceding chapter, only be satisfactorily determined for boys. Such analysis would involve cutting the number in each stream by half, a reduction which would make the numbers too small for the necessary calculations. For example in the top three streams of the grammar school, those for which this analysis would be most crucial, there is only one working-class boy who does not aspire to a middle-class job. He is number 21 in the 'C' stream, who is, as *Chart III* shows, a social isolate. Yet one can hardly make any generalizations from the case of this one unfortunate boy! We can only conclude, therefore, that the results of this study, as those of Oppenheim and Turner, give rise to the suggestion that, where positive educational selection has taken place, class of aspiration is a more important determinant of friendship preference than class of origin. But there is as yet no firm evidence to confirm or deny this hypothesis, and, given the size and homogeneity of the typical stream in the typical school, it is difficult to see how such evidence might be obtained.

Returning to the major hypothesis that '*Comprehensive school children will show less tendency to mix with children of their own social type than will tripartite schoolchildren*', there is no evidence whatever from this study of three schools that this is the case. In Cherry Dale as in most comprehensive schools, children are taught in doubly homogeneous social groups. They, like tripartite schoolchildren, mix during lesson time mainly with those from similar social background and those who are bound for similar eventual social status. The option for social mixing which is supposedly created in the comprehensive school by the house system is simply not taken up: children are more likely to choose their 'real friends' from their own academic streams than any others in the same school, and houses and house tutor groups have no impact on friendship formation. Within these homogeneous academic streams children apparently prefer to mix with those from similar social background.[26] Indeed even in the 'A' stream there is, among the middle class, considerable ingroup preference by class of origin (I.P. = 5·12). Since this is not so in the grammar school, one is tempted to consider the possibility that, for this academically successful group, 'the social effect of such schools is to reinforce rather than combat class consciousness'.[27] Had they gone to a grammar school would these children have been less 'class conscious' at least as far as *class background* is concerned? Is it possible that in this group 'children tend to underline and emphasize class differences from the very fear that they will become blurred'?[28]

NOTES

1   One of the first and certainly the best known expression of this view is in Waller, Willard, *The Sociology of Teaching*, New York, Wiley, 1932.

2   Hollingshead, August, *Elmtown's Youth*, New York, Wiley, 1949, pp. 204–42; Neugarten, Bernice, 'The Democracy of Childhood', in Warner, W. Lloyd, *Democracy in Jonesville*, New York, Harper, 1949, pp. 77–88; and, referring to older students, Lundberg, George, and Beazley, Virginia, 'Consciousness of Kind in a College Population', *Sociometry*, XI (1) (1948), pp. 59–74. Three other well known studies demonstrated small positive associations between father's occupation of choosers and chosen. Bonney, Merl E., 'A Sociometric Study of the Relationships of some Factor to Mutual Friendships on Elementary, Secondary and College Levels', *Sociometry*, 9 (1946), pp. 21–47; Dahlke, H. Otto, 'Determinants of Sociometric Relations among Children in the Elementary School', *loc. cit.*, 16 (1953), pp. 327–38; Potashin, Reva, 'A Sociometric Study of Children's Friendships', *loc. cit.*, IX (1946), pp. 48–70.

3 Oppenheim, A. N., 'Social Status and Clique Formation among Grammar School Boys', *Brit. Journ. Sociol.*, VI (1955), pp. 228–45.

4 Turner, Ralph, *The Social Context of Ambition*, Chandler, 1964, pp. 109–37.

5 *Ibid.*, p. 118.

6 For example, Crosland, C. A. R., *The Future of Socialism*, pp. 198–207; Pedley, Robin, *The Comprehensive School*, Pelican. 1963.

7 Davis, Robin, *The Grammar School*, Pelican, 1967, p. 157.

8 Pedley, *op. cit.*, p. 200.

9 Davis, *op. cit.*, p. 157. This problem was explicitly recognized in Circular 10/65 where Local Education Authorities are urged to ensure that catchment areas are as socially 'comprehensive' as possible, see *The Organisation of Secondary Education*, H.M.S.O. (1965).

10 This point is made by Corwin, Ronald G., *A Sociology of Education*, Meredith, 1965, pp. 140–2 for the American situation. There is a growing body of evidence that this homogenization is occurring in Britain. See for example Collison, Peter, 'Occupation, Education and Housing in an English City', *Amer. Journ. Sociol.*, LXV (6) (1960), pp. 588–97, and Pahl, R. E., *Urbanisation in Britain*, Longmans, forthcoming. This trend can also be seen in the residential patterns of new towns, see Heraud, B. J., 'Social Class and the New Towns', *Urban Studies*, V (1) (1968), pp. 33–58.

11 For summaries of the principle of house organization as a 'vertical' organization of the school see Pedley, *op. cit.*, pp. 122–7, and the Inner London Educational Authority publication: *London Comprehensive Schools*, I.L.E.A., 1967, pp. 132–47.

12 The interest here is in genuine friendship choice rather than preferences within a stipulated population, it was therefore considered that limitation to one choice was desirable in this case so that some of the artificiality engendered by the more traditional sociometric techniques might be avoided. The distinction between friendship *choice* and friendship *preference* is discussed further below where conventional sociometric techniques are also employed.

13 That is, if one assumes that most choices will be confined to the same year group (a not entirely realistic assumption) then the likelihood of making a choice within the same or an equivalent stream is approximately one in four in the grammar and comprehensive schools, and about one in three in the secondary modern. On this basis such choices in all schools occur at least

twice as often as one would expect by chance. And, when one includes the fact that the range from which choices are made is not in fact limited to the same year group these percentages can be seen to be even more significant. This finding corroborates Hargreaves' for his secondary modern school that 'In each form over half the boys selected as friends come from the same form. . . . Only in exceptional circumstances do friendship choices extend beyond one stream from the form of origin'. See Hargreaves, David H., *Social Relations in a Secondary School*, Routledge, 1967, p. 7.

14 Pape, G. V., article in *Forum*, CXI (2), pp. 7–9.

15 Young, Michael, and Armstrong, Michael, had suspected that, where academic streaming was practised, this would be the case. From observations they came to the conclusion that 'Children in the top streams mix mainly with other similar children, even in sports, and the houses are not much more than a place to leave your coat.' See 'The Flexible School', *Where*, supplement J, Autumn (1965), p. 4.

16 In other words there are empirical as well as theoretical reasons for accepting Parsons' characterization of the school class as the basic unit or social system within which the day-to-day facts of education and school social interaction takes place. See Parsons, Talcott, 'The School Class as a Social System', *Harvard Educational Review*, XXIX (1959), pp. 297–318.

17 See above, Chapter Three, *Table 3*.

18 This question was first used by Turner, *op. cit.*, p. 113.

19 At Cherry Dale school the initial intention had been to administer the sociometric questions to the children sitting as house tutor groups, for if the teachers were to be believed, these were the 'real' groups of the school. However, time-tabling of lessons would have been so badly upset by that arrangement that the children met as academic streams. In the light of the evidence presented above this was a most fortunate accident.

20 Turner, *op. cit.*, p. 113.

21 See, for example his *Who Shall Survive?*, Washington Nervous and Mental Disease Publishing Co., 1934.

22 It can also be seen initially that not all children gave three responses as requested, some being unable to name more than one (and one being unable to name any) individual who would be preferred as a friend. This fact does not, however, confuse the analysis as the statistical analysis of preferences which is presented later in this chapter was designed to cover a variable number of choices.

23 Note that while the immigrants make some choices of native children, only one of the latter chooses an immigrant. This exception (in Chart XIV: number 10 choosing 11) involved a middle-class Greek girl, the only immigrant in the stream who was not 'coloured'. The charts also draw attention to another feature of race relations in the school, the concentration of immigrants in the 'C' stream.

24 Proctor, C. H., and Loomis, C. P., 'Analysis of Sociometric Data', in Jahoda, Marie, Deutsch, Martin, and Cook, Stuart, (Eds.): *Research Methods in Social Relations*, Part II, N.Y. Dryden, 1951, p. 574. The formula for calculation of I.P. is as follows:

$$\text{I.P.} = \frac{\text{Ca-a (b)}}{\text{Ca-b (a-1)}}$$

Where: a = number of persons in ingroup
          b = number of persons in outgroup
          Ca-a = total number of choices directed by members of an ingroup to members of the same ingroup
          Ca-b = total number of choices directed by members of an ingroup to members of an outgroup.

25 In fact there is some evidence to suggest that working-class children in the grammar school tend to slip down-stream. Finally they concentrate in the 'D' stream where a more typically working-class subculture develops. See for example Jackson, B., and Marsden, D., *Education and the Working Class*, Routledge and Kegan Paul, 1962, and Dale, R., and Griffiths, S., *Downstream in the Grammar School*, Routledge, 1965.

26 Of course we have only examined stated preferences for hypothetical friendships which probably bear only indirectly on the concrete friendship patterns extant in the classroom. In order to examine 'real' friendships within the classroom it would be necessary to observe the groups constantly over a long period of time as did Hargreaves (*op. cit.*). Yet preferences for hypothetical friends are themselves social facts and they reveal something of the criteria by which children select their actual friends. For choice of friends like choice of jobs is a two-stage process, first preferences are established and then decisions are made on the basis of both these preferences *and* the perceived likelihood that the desire is reciprocal.

27 Koerner, James D., 'The Comprehensive Fallacy' in Davis, Robin, *op. cit.*, p. 263.

28 Davis, *ibid.*, p. 158.

6

Consciousness of Class

We have seen how the various forms of secondary education function to limit children's occupational horizons, and to effect a relative social segregation of the potential occupational 'successes' from the 'failures' – a segregation which mirrors that in the world outside school. Yet these phenomena are merely aspects of a broader process of selective socialization: they reveal two of the ways in which differential class consciousness, or more precisely *'consciousness of class'*,[1] is transmitted through the educational system. For one part of this consciousness consists in awareness of the existence of a class system based upon differences in occupational evaluations and the subsequent awareness of one's own place within it. We have seen in *Chapter 4* how the structural 'noise' of the school system[2] shapes children's self definitions and their consequent anticipations of adult status. In *Chapter 5* the development of a second element in this consciousness of class was examined, the way in which the organization of the school encourages the growth of informal social relationships along social class lines, thus perpetuating the social cleavages of class society. There is, however, a third component involved in the notion of consciousness of class. This is the idea usually covered by the more traditional expression 'class consciousness', and it refers to *ideologies* about social class.[3] It is with these class ideologies that the present chapter is concerned.

Precise definition of the term 'class ideology' naturally raises the problems involved in the definition of the term ideology itself. The present usage of the term does not entail any of the evaluative connotations given to it, for example, by Napoleon who used it as a pejorative for remote or impractical ideas, or Marx and Feurbach who used it to refer specifically to false bodies of thought, nor am I, like Mannheim limiting it to justifications of the *status quo*.[4] The notion of ideology employed here refers to a particular kind of 'definition of the situation', a special mode of ordering reality,[5] which both involves an emotional evaluation on the part of the believers and is consequential for their actions. This is close to the usage of Daniel Bell who uses terms such as 'a way of translating ideas into action', and 'the commitment to the consequences of ideas whose latent function is to tap emotion'.[6] Class ideologies then include ideas about the structure or shape of the class system together with evaluations of its legitimacy and values and norms relating to class behaviour, particularly those defining possibility and/or desirability of social mobility.

The way in which the organization of the educational system affects differential socialization into class ideologies is a crucial feature of a stratified society. For the distribution of ideologies about the class system is an 'objective' characteristic of that system[7] as important in its consequences as the distribution of physical resources and life chances and the rates of social mobility. Class ideology is no mere epiphenomenon of social class but 'reacts upon the objective conditions to which it refers and has ramifying effects upon directly and indirectly related features of the society'.[8]

In a well-known paper[9] Ralph Turner has suggested a major way in which the organization of formal education is related to class ideologies. He distinguishes two ideal-typical organizing folk norms which may define the accepted mode of upward mobility in a class society.

On the one hand, mobility may be viewed as most appropriately a *contest* in which many contestants strive by whatever combinations of strategy, enterprise, perseverance and ability they can marshal, restricted only by a minimum set of rules defining fair play and minimising special advantage of those who get ahead early in the game, to take possession of a limited number of prizes. On the other hand it may be thought best that the upwardly mobile person be *sponsored*, like one who joins a private club upon the invitation of the membership, selected because the club members feel that he has the qualities desirable in a club member, and then subjected to careful training and initiation into the guiding ethic and lore of the club before being accorded full membership.[10]

The 'contest' ideology is seen as prevailing where the educational system operates to delay selection as long as possible and to minimize social differentiation in the schools. Thus the comprehensive system of secondary education in the United States is accompanied by a popular tendency to view the acceptable mode of mobility as one in keeping with the idea of a competition, for 'the logic of preparation for a contest prevails in United States schools, with emphasis on keeping everyone in the running until the final stages.'[11]

The early selection characteristic of English tripartite education can, on the other hand, be seen as producing a prevalence of 'sponsored' mobility ideologies.[12] In our ideal-typical comprehensivists' theory it is proposed that where premature educational segregation produces narrowed occupational horizons and class-based social relationships, children's perceptions of the structure and meaning of stratification will take the form of rigid dichotomous models: they will see the class structure as relatively closed, consisting of those who have been 'chosen' or 'ordained' and those who have not. On the other hand replacement of tripartite by comprehensive secondary schools is viewed as reversing the situation and it is hypothesized that *Comprehensive school children will tend to have views of the class system as a flexible hierarchy, while tripartite school children will tend to see this as a rigid dichotomy.'*[13]

The popular classification of class ideologies as 'power' or 'prestige' models[15] is also one which, while referring explicitly to evaluations of the class system and notions of the possibility of social mobility within it, simultaneously includes a dimension of perception of the *shape* of that system. Thus the concept of a 'power' model covers the view of the class structure as a 'non-avertable dichotomy'[16] (or at least one which is avertable only by radical collective action), while that of a prestige model describes a view of the class structure as a hierarchy containing at least three ranks between which individuals may move fairly freely according to their ability and motivation. The suggestion that comprehensive schooling will effect a shift away from rigid dichotomous class ideologies towards flexible hierarchic ones, then implies a change in both perceptions of the shape of the class system and notions about its legitimacy, particularly as those are expressed in ideas about possible modes of social mobility.

For the purposes of the present analysis, then, class ideologies can be classified on two dimensions. In the first place perceptions of the shape of the class order may be distinguished according to the number of strata which the subjects conceptualize. Obviously the number of gradations employed may range from the simple dichotomy of 'us' and 'them' reported by Hoggart[17] to the fine distinctions between classes and subclasses employed in some of the early American community studies.[18] However in the present case it is necessary only to distinguish dichotomous views from those making use of three or more categories, for it can be argued that as soon as individuals begin to conceive of society as containing more than two great sections, 'those up there' and 'the rest of us', they have some, albeit primitive, notion of hierarchy.[19]

A second dimension on which class ideologies may be classified concerns evaluations of the legitimacy of the *status quo* as these are expressed in ideas about possible and desirable modes of social mobility. Individuals may on the one hand consider social class divisions as illegitimate and therefore rule out the possibility of individual social mobility within the system, seeing the only possibility for social change in collective action. On the other hand they may consider the distribution of status and its correlates in society to be quite fair since advantages are gained by those who, as a result of their own efforts, deserve them. On this view of course individual social mobility is seen as both possible and highly desirable.[20]

Cross-classification of these two dimensions yields four types of class ideology.

Typology of Class Ideologies
Evaluation of the legitimacy of the class structure

		ILLEGITIMATE	LEGITIMATE
	DICHOTOMY	1 'Power' Models	2 'Deference' Models
Perception of the shape of the class structure	HIERARCHY	3 Instrumental-Collectivist' Models	4 'Prestige' Models

The first type is the traditional working-class ideology as described by the orthodox Marxist notion of class consciousness. Such models rest on the notion of a basic cleavage in society which cannot be ameliorated without revolutionary social change. Bott notes that in her sample of 'ordinary urban families' these models 'were used by people who identified themselves strongly with the working class and felt no desire or compulsion to be socially mobile. They conceived classes as interdependent or conflicting groups; their idea of bettering their position was by organizing the working class to get more out of the bosses'.[21]

Models of the second type resemble power models in that they too involve notions of the class system as a dichotomous structure, however in this case the dichotomy is seen as legitimate. Still society is seen in terms of 'them' and 'us', but in this case 'they' are not targets for hostility but models for emulation. Our knowledge of this form of social imagery derives mainly from studies of the 'deference voter'.[22] It seems that the deferential syndrome may involve elements of seemingly contradictory beliefs. For individuals using this form of stratification map usually recognize the importance of ascriptive criteria in the maintenance of a hereditary elite, yet they somehow manage to maintain the view that this elite *deserves* its favoured position. This is accompanied by the belief that anyone can, through personal effort, attain recognition by the elite and thus achieve social mobility,[23] while those who are not motivated to 'do their best' are looked down upon along with other 'lumpen' proletarians such as 'spongers' and the unemployed.[24]

Conceptualization of the third type of class ideology, the instrumental-collectivist orientation, entails a significant departure from the more traditional classifications of social class imagery. Bott, for example, argues that 'the use of two basic classes is a logical consequence of using the ideas of power, conflict and opposition, since two units represent the smallest number required for conflict'.[25] But a view of the class structure as an illegitimate *hierarchy* is not only logically possible but empirically common. Mallet in France and Goldthorpe and Lockwood in England have described the class views of a rising group of workers, the relatively highly skilled and highly paid proletariat.[26] These workers have a somewhat sophisticated view of the shape of the class structure, because they clearly differentiate themselves from the very poor, the unskilled and the unemployed but do not necessarily see themselves as middle class.[27] Yet their relative good fortune does not result in a view of this hierarchy as a legitimate order, but rather in a sensation of relative deprivation which in turn produces a radical and negative stance towards class society. This radicalism is not, however, based upon rejection of the class order in *principle* so much as a pragmatic and instrumental rejection of the present order. They see collective action as an efficient means of status equilibration, aiming to raise their general prestige to a level more congruent with their financial position, through union and political activities.

The final type of class ideology is that which has been frequently labelled the 'prestige' model. On this view differential status and reward are legitimately ranked in a hierarchy, the most deserving individuals receiving the largest material and symbolic rewards. This is the most basic expression of the Western democratic ideal, an elaboration of the notion of an open contest which Turner has described. The child who, when asked 'How does a boss become a boss?', replied 'Because he's been good at work, and when they're good at working they got to be a boss',[28] was expressing this view.

The comprehensive ideal is, of course, itself an expression of this fourth type of class ideology. Liberal optimists whose own ideological perspectives lead them to see their societies as fluid hierarchies generally attribute a crucial role to comprehensive education in the maintenance of this democracy. For, as Corwin has pointed out, probably the majority of educators and citizens in America 'believe that the comprehensive school is THE most appropriate in a democracy society'.[29] Using a similar logic liberal critics of the British system of education see segregated secondary schools as stemming from and perpetuating the rigid dichotomous class system.[30] They believe that, in so far as the daily facts of social class are those of face-to-face acceptance and rejection, solidarity and hostility, and situational superiority and inferiority, then educational reform may result in social reform as future citizens are produced who hold 'democratic' rather than rigid 'antagonistic' class ideologies.

It has been said that 'reliance on education as a means of

improving the world may be so popular because it seems to be a safe way to institute change: when stressing the potential of education eventually to change individuals, reformers need not concern themselves with the dreadful prospect of altering entrenched social structures.'[31] Yet ideological 'exposure' of liberal reformers can be no substitute for actual examination of their hypothesis. Let us therefore examine the evidence for the view that among comprehensive school children class ideologies of the fourth type ('Prestige' models) will predominate, while among tripartite schoolchildren dominant ideologies will be of the first type ('Power') models.

In order to operationalize and measure the dimensions of the typology of class ideologies a number of attitude scales were employed. The children were required to indicate the truth or falsity of eight statements about social class on five-point scales, and their responses were combined to produce indices of perceptions and evaluations of the class structure.[32] On the basis of these two indices each child's class imagery could then be classified as one of the four types. Nineteen per cent of the respondents held 'Power' models, 23 per cent 'Deference' models, 30 per cent 'Instrumental Collective' models and 29 per cent 'Prestige' models.

When the distribution of these four types of class imagery by school experience was examined, controlling for social class origin and sex, the patterns presented in *Table 6.1* were revealed.

In the first place it is apparent that class ideologies are related to 'objective' social class in the way which is implied in the definition of the four ideal types of class ideology. Thus nearly one quarter of the working-class boys have 'Power' models, while only 12 per cent of middle-class boys do so, yet nearly one half of the middle-class boys and only 19 per cent of the working-class boys have 'Prestige' models. Similarly the third type of class ideology, the 'Instrumental Collective' model, is slightly more frequent among the working-class than the middle-class boys. This relationship between 'objective' social class and class imagery as it is here defined is not, of course, perfect although it is statistically significant ($X^2 = 11\cdot7$, $d.f. = 3$, $p = \cdot01$). However as Sugarman has said '"social class" is just a shorthand way of referring to a complex of factors which correlate with occupation',[33] what we really mean by social class is not father's

TABLE 6.1

Class Ideologies by School Type, Sex and Social Class Background

	CLASS IDEOLOGY				
	1 'Power' %	2 'Defer-ence' %	3 'Instru-mental Collective' %	4 'Prestige' %	N = (100%)
WORKING CLASS BOYS					
Grammar	24	18	24	35	17
Comp. 'A' stream	25	17	33	25	12
Comp. 'B'–'D' streams	24	27	31	18	51
Sec. Modern	25	33	33	8	24
Total	24	26	31	19	104
WORKING CLASS GIRLS					
Grammar	8	17	33	41	12
Comp. 'A' stream	9	9	36	45	11
Comp. 'B'–'D' streams	13	17	42	27	47
Sec. Modern	25	32	18	25	28
Total	15	20	34	31	98
MIDDLE CLASS BOYS					
Grammar	9	24	18	48	33
Comp. 'A' stream	17	8	25	50	12
Comp. 'B'–'D' streams	17	17	33	33	6
Sec. Modern	14	28	43	14	7
Total	12	21	24	43	58
MIDDLE CLASS GIRLS					
Grammar	17	23	31	28	35
Comp. 'A' stream	25	0	25	50	4
Comp. 'B'–'D' streams	22	22	22	33	9
Sec. Modern	25	25	17	33	12
Total	20	22	27	32	60

320

occupation but a complex of values and norms of which parental occupational prestige is merely a crude indicator. Thus the lack of a perfect correlation between class background and class ideology as these are used here may result as much from error in the measurement of the former as imprecise operationalization of the latter.

A second observation which can be made about *Table 6.1* is the difference between boys and girls. For example, whereas only 19 per cent of working-class boys hold 'Prestige' models, nearly one third of the girls from the same class background do so, and the girls are less inclined than the boys to hold 'Power' models. This is probably a result of the frequently observed tendency for females to hold more conservative social and political attitudes,[34] and for this reason as well as those expounded in Chapter 4 it seems reasonable to treat girls separately from boys with regard to investigating the relationship between school experience and class ideologies.

Considering boys only then, it is only in the grammar school that a majority see the class structure as legitimate (second and fourth models) for in the comprehensive and secondary modern schools conceptions of social class as illegitimate are more dominant. In *Table 6.2* the vertical dimension of the typology is collapsed to show this trend.

TABLE 6.2

Boys Only: Evaluations of the Legitimacy of the Class Structure

| | CLASS STRUCTURE SEEN AS: | | |
By School Experience	*Legitimate* (Models 2 & 4) %	*Illegitimate* (Models 1 & 3) %	N = (100%)
Grammar	67	33	50
Comprehensive 'A' stream	50	50	24
Comprehensive 'B'–'D' streams	46	54	57
Secondary Modern	42	58	31
N =	84	78	162

Thus, while when grammar school boys are compared with the rest the differences in evaluations of the class structure are statistically significant ($X^2 = 5.7$, $d.f. = 1$, $p = .05$), comprehensive school boys do not differ significantly from secondary modern school boys ($X^2 = 0.21$, $d.f. = 1$, $p = $ n.s.), and, when all the tripartite schoolboys are compared with all the comprehensive schoolboys there are again no significant differences ($X^2 = 1.14$, $d.f. = 1$, $p = $ n.s.). Thus there is no evidence to support the view that 'eliminating the Eleven-Plus and the move toward comprehensive education will increase the role of the education system as a legitimiser of the stratification system',[35] at least for the present sample. Indeed, one might tentatively suggest the opposite, for *Table 6.2* shows that those comprehensively educated boys who might, under tripartite, have attended grammar schools (that is the 'A' stream) have *evaluations* of the class structure more similar to the lower stream boys in their own school, and the secondary modern school boys, than to those boys who actually attend a grammar school.

The hypothesized movement along the other dimension of the typology, from dichotomous to hierarchic models of social class, can also be investigated by analysis of *Table 6.1*. By collapsing together the first and second versus the third and fourth models we can examine the relative frequency of dichotomous and hierarchic conceptions for the four types of schooling. The results of this comparison are shown in *Table 6.3*.

TABLE 6.3
Boys Only: Perceptions of the Shape of the Class Structure by School Experience

| | CLASS STRUCTURE SEEN AS: | | |
	Dichotomy (Models 1 & 2) %	Hierarchy (Models 3 & 4) %	N = (100%)
Grammar	36	64	50
Comprehensive 'A' stream	33	66	24
Comprehensive 'B'–'D' streams	49	51	57
Secondary Modern	55	45	31
	71	91	162

Table 6.3 shows that while comprehensive school boys do not differ from tripartite schoolboys on this dimension ($X^2 = \cdot04$, *d.f.* $= 1$, $p =$ n.s.) there are some interesting differences when the whole range of educational experience is considered. For comprehensive school children are polarized in a way reflecting the pattern for tripartite schoolchildren: those who are positively 'selected' under either system being more likely to see the class system as a hierarchy than the less fortunate ($X^2 = 4\cdot67$, *d.f.* $= 1$, $p = \cdot05$). This same trend, for the comprehensive 'A' stream boys to resemble grammar school boys and the compre-

hensive lower stream boys to resemble secondary modern school boys, can also be observed in *Table 6.4* where the distribution of 'Prestige' models is considered alone.

TABLE 6.4

Boys Only: Distribution of Prestige Models by Type of Schooling

	Prestige Models (model 4) %	N = (100%)
Grammar	44	50
Comprehensive 'A' stream	37	24
Comprehensive 'B'–'D' streams	19	57
Secondary Modern	10	31
N=	45	162

When 'selective' (Grammar and Comprehensive 'A' stream) is compared with 'non-selective' schooling ($X^2 = 12.49$, $d.f. = 1$, $p = .001$).

In sum, there is no evidence from *Table 6.1* or *Table 6.2, 6.3* and *6.4*, which are derived from it, to indicate that comprehensive schooling produces a movement in children's class ideologies in either of the directions predicted by the theory. Conceptions of the class structure as a legitimate hierarchy are no more frequent among comprehensive school children than tripartite schoolchildren. Indeed, although the numbers involved in the present analysis are too small to permit partial correlations, it does appear that the most important influence on children's class ideologies is not education but objective class background. In so far as education does play a part in determining children's notions about social class, however, it appears to do so through overt selection whether this takes place under a tripartite or a so-called comprehensive system. Those who have been, as it were, vindicated by the system through positive selection for grammar school or comprehensive school 'A' stream tend, naturally to view the class system as a flexible hierarchy ('Prestige' models) more often than those who have not. Similarly model Three, the other hierarchical model, is more frequent among the 'selected'. However, curiously, *evaluations* do not exhibit a clear trend in this direction (all comprehensive school children tending to behave similarly to the secondary modern school children) but this may simply reflect the small numbers of comprehensive 'A' stream boys.

Now the reader might reasonably object that it is all too easy to demonstrate that two factors are *not* related together, especially when one of them is synthetic. Clearly individual cases can be classified on any two dichotomized variables to produce four types. That one can fill all four cells of a two-by-two typology is therefore in no way a validation of that typology. And that one can show that these four types are not related to some third factor could be interpreted as demonstrating no more than that the classification is completely random and the so-called indices measure nothing at all! It is therefore necessary to introduce independent evidence to show that the typology of class ideologies is a meaningful classification representing real differences between respondents' perceptions and evaluations of their social worlds.

One way in which this can be done is to introduce subsidiary hypotheses, relationships which could be expected to obtain if the classification of class ideologies were genuine. The following two hypotheses were considered:

6 Children who are potentially mobile are more likely to hold a 'Prestige' model than those who are not.
7 Children holding 'Power' and 'Instrumental-Collective' models are less likely to accept the bases of status allocation in society than those with 'Deference' and 'Prestige' models.

The first of these subsidiary hypotheses is based upon the assumption that individuals who are likely to be socially mobile and who anticipate such mobility cannot reasonably hold a view of society as either rigid or dichotomous. In order to entertain the notion of personal mobility one must typically perceive the class structure as a legitimate hierarchy in which positions are allocated on the basis of relevant attributes. In order to test this hypothesis the Index of Aspiration Increment was employed. As in Chapter 4 the working-class boys were divided into three groups according to their Index score, and those who were potentially highly mobile were compared with those with more modest mobility aspirations and with the stable and downwardly mobile. The results are shown in *Table 6.5.*

It is clear from the table that class ideology is related to mobility aspirations. Children aspiring to move out of the working class do tend to see class society in open competitive terms (well over a third hold 'Prestige' models compared with only 28 per cent holding both the dichotomous models put together). Among the non-mobile, on the other hand, 'Power' and 'Deference' models are most frequent and only 9 per cent

TABLE 6.5

Working Class Boys Only:
Index of Aspiration Increment by Class Ideologies

	Class Ideology				
	1 'Power' %	2 'Deference' %	3 'Instru- mental Collective' %	4 'Prestige' %	N = (100%)
Index of Aspiration Increment					
1–2 (highly mobile, aspiring to middle class)	19	19	26	36	42
3–4 (mobile within the work- ing class)	20	28	45	8	40
5 (stable and downwardly mobile)	41	36	14	9	22
Total	24	26	31	19	104

$(X^2 = 23 \cdot 03, \ d.f. = 6, \ p = \cdot 001)$

hold 'Prestige' models. The importance of the third type of class ideology for those who aspire to mobility within the working class is interesting and tends to support the notion that this 'Instrumental Collective' type of class ideology is predominant among the rising skilled worker group.

Hypothesis Seven follows from the definition of the horizontal dimension of the typology. For those who accept the class structure as legitimate are likely to see the bases of allocation of positions as reasonable and acceptable. In order to obtain an independent measure of acceptance of the basic criteria of status allocation, then, children were asked 'Imagine that one of your friends is applying for a job as a junior manager in a store. What do you think will be the most important things which will be taken into consideration in deciding whether or not he should get the job?' They were then required to rank six items covering personal achievement ('How many 'O' levels he has'), ascriptive attributes, ('The sort of accent he has'), and irrelevances ('What his hobbies are'). They were then asked to rank the same items, considering this time which characteristics they considered *should* be employed as criteria.[36] The 'fit' between the two sets of rankings thus provided a measure of the extent to which the children *accepted* the criteria of job allocation which they perceived to be operative in society. Respondents were divided into 'Acceptors' and 'Rejectors' on this basis[37] and the class ideologies of the two groups were compared.

TABLE 6.6

Boys Only:

Acceptance of Perceived Bases of Job Allocation by Class Ideologies

	Class Ideology				
	I 'Power' %	2 'Deference' %	3 'Instru- mental Collective' %	4 'Prestige' %	N = (100%)
'Acceptors'	16	30	22	33	95
'Rejectors'	25	16	38	21	67
	20	24	29	28	162

It can be seen from *Table 6.6* that, although in the sample of boys there is a general tendency to accept rather than reject the perceived bases of job allocation, this is related to class ideology in the expected directions. More of the 'Acceptors' have 'Prestige' or 'Deference' models, while more of the 'Rejectors' have 'Power' and 'Instrumental-Collective' models. ($X^2 = 9.45$, $d.f. = 1, p = .01$).

Tables 6.5 and *6.6* then give some indication that the typology of class ideologies and its operationalization are empirically justified. When this evidence is taken together with the observation (from *Table 6.1*) that class ideologies are related to 'objective' social class in the manner one would expect, it seems reasonable to conclude that this classification of class imagery is indeed a reflection of real differences in world views among the respondents.

Yet, while there appears to have been some success in the operationalization and measurement of class imagery, there is certainly no evidence from the present study that reorganization of secondary education along comprehensive lines will affect this imagery in the manner envisaged in *Hypothesis Five*. Of course this is hardly surprising, for it is proposed in the theory that comprehensive schooling will produce a widening of children's occupational horizons and a relative decline in within-class informal social interaction, and that *as a result* their class ideologies will tend to change from 'Power' to 'Prestige' models. Since, as we have seen, there is no evidence that either aspirations or informal social relations are affected by comprehensive schooling, the findings presented in the present chapter serve merely to underline those of the preceding two. For consciousness of class, as this is manifest in aspirations, interactions and subjective models of stratified society, persists in the comprehensive as in the grammar and secondary modern schools.

In this light such colourful optimism as Crosland was expressing only a decade ago turns a whiter shade of pale.

The system will increasingly, if the Labour Party does its job, be built around the comprehensive school. . . . All schools will more and more be socially mixed; all will provide routes to the Universities and to every type of occupation, from the highest to the lowest. . . . Then, very slowly, Britain may cease to be the most class-ridden country in the world![38]

NOTES

1   I use this rather in the way in which Touraine uses 'conscience de classe' although this is often translated as class consciousness. That he is using it in a sense broader than the traditional 'class consciousness' is clear when he says '. . . parce que les éléments qui constituent cette conscience de classe peuvent ne pas se

trouver tous reunis; il peut se faire qu'un groupe ouvrier ait une vive conscience de lui-même, sans avoir ni une conscience hostile au groupe patronal, ni une vision de la société comme commandée par la lutte des classes...'. Touraine, Alain, *La Conscience Ouvriere*, Editions du Seuil, Paris, 1966, p. 16.

2   William Taylor has pointed out that school operates to shape children's expectations less through *explicit* messages than through what in communications theory is called 'noise'. See his 'Secondary Reorganization and the Transition from School to Work' in *Aspects of Education*, No. V, p. 91.

3   Lionel S. Lewis has suggested that in contemporary writing there are *five* different meanings of the term 'class consciousness' to be found. The three senses employed here represent a re-grouping of his types. See 'Class Consciousness and Inter-Class Sentiments', *Sociological Quarterly*, VI (1965), pp. 325–38.

4   Bottomore provides a useful summary of the various definitions of the term in his article. 'Some Reflections on the Sociology of Knowledge', *Brit. Journ. Sociol*, VII (1956), pp. 52–8. See also Mannheim, Karl, *Ideology and Utopia*, Routledge & Kegan Paul, 1936; and Lichtheim, George, 'The Concepts of Ideology' in Nadel, George H., *Studies in the Philosophy of History*, Harper, 1965, pp. 148–79, where another useful history of the usage of the concept is provided.

5   Berger and Luckman also take the position that ideology is a special kind of definition of the situation, but for them only 'when a particular definition of reality *comes to be attached to a concrete power interest* it may be called an ideology'. See Berger, Peter, and Luckman, Thomas, *The Social Construction of Reality*, Allen Lane, Penguin, 1967. A problem with this is that elements of the same 'concrete power interest' may entertain different ideologies, thus deferential workers share the same concrete power interests as traditional radical ones yet would their definition of the class structure be termed an ideology?

6   Bell, Daniel, *The End of Ideology*, Collier, 1961, pp. 393–5.

7   I am using 'objective' here in the sense in which it is employed by Berger and Luckman. Of course distributions of ideologies are not *physically* things but they are objective in the sense that they compose the symbolic universe which is, for any individual 'out there', or as Durkheim has put it 'external and constraining'. See Berger and Luckman, *op. cit.*, pp. 110–46, and Parsons, Talcott, *The Structure of Social Action*, Glencoe Free Press, 1964, pp. 378–90.

8   Turner, Ralph, 'Modes of Social Ascent Through Education:

Sponsored and Contest Mobility', *Amer. Sociol. Rev.* (1960), reprinted in Halsey, A. H., *et al.*, *Education, Economy and Society*, Free Press Glencoe, 1961, p. 122.

9   *Op. cit.*, pp. 121–39.

10   *Ibid.*, pp. 135–6.

11   *Ibid.*, p. 131.

12   It should be noted that Turner does not explicitly suggest that the organization of schooling *causes* the development of the particular type of mobility ideology. Indeed he states that he is not concerned with *how* the systems became what they are but merely with their continued functioning. However the implication of causality is contained in the theory under examination here.

13   Turner himself suggests the possibility of this development when he argues that the introduction of comprehensive secondary schools in England may 'dull the distinctive edge of the sponsorship system' (p. 137). Yet he adds: 'It remains to be determined whether the comprehensive school in England will take a distinctive form and serve a distinctive function that preserves the pattern of sponsorship or whether it will approximate to the present American system.'

14   *The Social Context of Ambition*, Chandler, 1964, especially pp. 46–9.

15   A useful summary-description of these ideal types can be found in Goldthorpe, John H., and Lockwood, David, 'Affluence and the British Class Structure', *Sociological Review*, II (1963), pp. 133–63 where most of the literature on social class imagery is also cited.

16   See Popitz, H., *et al.*, *Das Gesellschaftsbild des Arbeiters*, 2nd edn., Teubingen, 1961.

17   Hoggart, Richard, *The Uses of Literacy*, Pelican, 1958, especially Chapter 4.

18   See for example, Warner, W. L., and Lunt, P. S., *The Social Life of a Modern Community*, New Haven, Yale University Press, 1941, and Davis, A., Gardner, B. B. and Gardner, M. R., *Deep South*, Chicago University Press, 1941.

19   Dahrendorf notes how, where dichotomous perceptions prevail, there are popular expressions to denote the two classes: '*them* and *us* in Britain, *ceux qui sont en haut* and *en bas* in Switzerland (and probably in France), *die da oben* and *wir heir unten* in Germany – these are expressions which belong to the stock-in-trade of working-class language'. Dahrendorf, Ralph, *Class and Class Conflict in Industrial Society*, Routledge, 1965, p. 285.

Touraine also treats hierarchic perceptions homogeneously as including all those using three or more strata. *Op. cit.*, p. 158.

20 Of course reduction of the variation in class ideologies to these two simple dimensions represents an enormous oversimplification. It may be argued, for example, that *evaluations* of the class system are not unidimensional. For while I have referred to notions of legitimacy 'as they are expressed in' ideas about the possibility and desirability of social mobility, one might well argue that these are two separate dimensions. Certainly if we were considering the ideologies of caste and estate systems as well as those of class we would have to include the conception of the system as legitimate but which entertains no personal notion of social mobility. By the same token the cynical attitude whereby the class system is rejected as illegitimate but personal mobility within it is seen as desirable, is both logically possible and probably does occur empirically. However, as we shall see, in this case ideas about legitimacy and personal mobility were *empirically* coincident in the manner suggested by the typology so, in the context of the present problem the classification employed was considered justified.

21 Bott, Elizabeth, *Family and Social Network*, Tavistock, 1964, pp. 175. Dahrendorf also notes the importance of this kind of model: he states that 'Even at a time when revolutionary ideologies of the Marxist type have lost their grip on workers everywhere, there remains an image of society which, in its political consequences, is incompatible with the more harmonious image of those "above", whether they be called "capitalists", "ruling class" or even "middle class" '. *Op. cit.*, p. 284.

22 For good accounts of the social imagery of deference voters see Samuel, R., 'The Deference Voter', *New Left Review*, January (1960), and Stacey, Margaret, *Tradition and Change*, Oxford, 1960.

23 On this belief 'individual mobility does not directly lead to social mobility. But it can lead to recognition by those with higher status that this achievement should be rewarded. It . . . thus leads indirectly to social mobility', Crutchley, John F., *Work Situations and Social Imagery*, Mimeo., Enfield College, London, 1967.

24 My location of traditional deferential working-class images as notions of legitimate dichotomy differs from that of Lockwood who states 'the model of society held by the deferential worker is a prestige or hierarchical, rather than a power or dichotomous model.' See Lockwood, D., 'Sources of Variation in Working

Class Images of Society', *Sociological Review*, XIV (3) (1966), p. 252; also Crutchley, *op. cit.*, p. 6. This is because this type is seen here as both logically and empirically distinct from the 'prestige model'. However, 'objectively' working-class individuals holding 'prestige' models may well vote Conservative, and would therefore on the traditional definition, be designated deferential. It seems likely that 'deferential *voters*' can hold either the second or the fourth type of class imagery.

25 Bott, *op. cit.*, p. 175. Willener also considers that the notion of dichotomy and that of conflict are inextricably bound together yet while Bott considers that the idea of conflict leads on to the notion of dichotomy Willener considers that the notion of dichotomy implies antagonism. See Willener, Alfred, *Images de la Société et Classes Sociales*, Bern, 1957, p. 206.

26 See Goldthorpe, John, and Lockwood, David, *op. cit.*, and Mallet, S., *La Nouvelle Classe Ouvriere*, Paris, Ed. du Seuil, 1963, pp. 143–76, also Anderson, Perry, in Anderson and Blackburn Robin, (Eds.), *Towards Socialism*, Collins, 1965, pp. 221–90.

27 In fact Goldthorpe and Lockwood's analysis suggests that questions requiring subjects to locate themselves as working or middle class, etc. may be meaningless or at least highly ambiguous. Where subjects have a sophisticated, sometimes multidimensional, view of the class system subjective class identification is less interesting than the nature of the social imagery involved. As Kahl has said, 'we must go back to the public with more flexible questions which allow respondents to choose both the model and their position within it', Kahl, J. A., *The American Class Structure*, Holt, Rinehart & Winston, 1965, p. 181.

28 Davies, A. F., 'The Child's Discovery of Social Class', *Australian and New Zealand Journ. of Sociology*, (1) (1967), pp. 21–37.

29 Corwin, Ronald G., *A Sociology of Education*, Meredith, 1965, p. 140.

30 The implication here is that in class ideology if not in class structure (that is 'objective' life chances) the American stratification system is more 'open' and is based on achievement whereas the British class system is relatively 'closed' and based on ascription. This is, of course, not a statement of agreed sociological fact but a highly controversial opinion. However the positions taken by American sociologists have tended to emphasize a common core of shared values (see for the most obvious example Merton's notion of anomie in Merton, R. K., *Social Theory and Social Structure*, Free Press 1957, 2nd edn.,)

while British sociologists have tended to emphasize the value-distinctness of social classes. In his *The Delinquent Solution*, Routledge, 1966, David Downes, for example examines the distribution of values in London working class boys and concludes that they have not internalized 'common' middle-class values.

31 Corwin, *op. cit.*, p. 57, discussing Lester Ward's view in *Dynamic Sociology*, II, New York (1883).

32 For details of the operationalization of the typology and construction of indices see *Appendix Four*.

33 Sugarman, B. N., 'Social Class and Values as Related to Achievement and Conduct in School', *Sociol. Rev.*, XIV (3) (1966), pp. 287–301.

34 See for example Blondel, J., *Voters, Parties and Leaders*, Pelican 1965, p. 60.

35 Abramson, Paul R., 'English Secondary Education and the Political Socialization Process', *Sociology of Education*, XL (3) (1967), p. 254.

36 The verbal instruction accompanying this question invited the children to imagine that *they* were the prospective employers. Thus the criteria they considered *should* be employed meant those that they would themselves employ.

37 'Actual' and 'ideal' rankings for each item were compared and any individuals differing by more than *two* ranks on any *one* item were designated as rejecting the operative criteria.

38 Crosland, C. A. R., *The Future of Socialism*, Cape 1963, first published in 1956, p. 207.

7

Towards Utopia?

What, then, are the chances of comprehensive reorganization of secondary education bringing closer the Utopia we seem to be seeking? How far will such educational reform produce the 'Fairer Society'? What hope is there that comprehensive education will reduce the salience of social class in this society?

This study of three London schools has failed to produce support for any of the five hypotheses derived from the theory suggested in Chapter 1. The so-called *educational* arguments still rage on; it will take large scale longitudinal research to produce definite answers to the questions of whether comprehensive education will produce a greater development of talent, or even improve the chances of equality of opportunity for those with equal talent. But many people believe that, even in the absence of conclusive proof of the educational case for comprehensive reorganization, the *social* arguments are indisputable. Yet we have seen that there is no evidence from this study to suggest that we can expect any of the three hypothesized 'social' effects of comprehensivization. In the comprehensive school, as in the tripartite schools, children learn early what level they can expect to achieve in the occupational structure, they are in this respect conscious of the class nature of the society in which they live. Their consciousness of class is also expressed in their informal associations at school, for the comprehensive school fails to neutralize the impact of class background and anticipated social class on children's friendship patterns. Their perceptions and evaluations of the class system also remain unaffected by comprehensive education. There is no evidence that children come to think of the stratification system as a fluid legitimate hierarchy, rather than an inevitable and illegitimate dichotomy, as a result of comprehensive schooling. There is, in short, no *evidence* that comprehensive education contributes to the breaking down of the barriers of social class which still divide adults and children alike.

But does this mean that comprehensive reorganization is not worth pursuing, that the system of segregated secondary schools which has existed for over twenty years should be maintained? There are, in fact, three possible interpretations of the results of this study, and they suggest three quite different imperatives for educational policy.

In the first place it might be suggested that Cherry Dale School is not a typical comprehensive school and therefore that the only policy conclusion that can be drawn from the data presented in the preceding chapters is that more research needs to be done on comprehensive schools. On one level, of course, this might be a trivial statement, like the assertion by a headmaster that 'There is no typical comprehensive school', because they are all different,[1] for scientists have never denied the uniqueness of each individual instance of a phenomenon. They merely maintain that, in order to understand, predict, and perhaps eventually control, what happens in the world, we have to make generalizations. To assert that each school is different is tantamount to arguing that we might as well give up doing scientific research in the sphere of education and merely collect vast libraries of information about all these different schools.

But it is certainly valid to ask whether Cherry Dale is really typical in another sense. For if this school were unlike the majority of comprehensive schools in relevant aspects of its organization or intake then the extent to which generalization could be made from the present study would be severely limited. We have already seen that Cherry Dale school was deliberately chosen for its untypicality in one respect: it is virtually uncreamed. Yet this is a condition which favours support of the theory rather than the opposite. For if no support can be found for the hypotheses in this virtually uncreamed school, it is extremely doubtful that such support would be found in creamed schools!

However, even though, as we have seen in *Chapter 4*, the social class and ability composition of the Cherry Dale intake was comparable to that of the tripartite schools, there might still be some respect in which the Cherry Dale neighbourhood differs from that of most other comprehensives. By considering only one comprehensive school, one might argue, the importance of 'neighbourhood context' has been ignored.[2]

It is certainly true that Cherry Dale School, unlike some other schools, stands on a housing estate, and that the area is dominantly working class. We have seen how a comprehensive school in a working-class area compares with tripartite schools in similar areas, yet perhaps in middle-class areas comprehensive schools compare more favourably with tripartite schools. But then the majority of areas, like the majority of children, *are* working class. And it is, after all, with the plight of the working-class children that educational reformers have been primarily concerned.

But this does not mean that further research is unnecessary! For small studies like this one can never be more than pointers to the need for research on a grander scale. It has already been suggested that the 'educational' questions cannot be answered until national longitudinal studies have been carried out, but it is also true that more conclusive answers to the 'social' questions can only be obtained from studies of a number of schools in different neighbourhoods with varying intake resources. Indeed if one firm policy recommendation can be made on the basis of this study it is that the first step towards improvement of secondary education is not a blind pursuance of comprehensive reorganization but adequate research into the likely effects of such reorganization. What *is* certain is that we have no grounds for certainty that the continuation of the present policy of comprehensivization will produce any of the supposed results.

A second conclusion one might draw from the failure to support the hypotheses is that education is not an independent variable. One might argue, as did Warner,[3] that the notion that social structures can be changed through educational reform is a liberal myth. For schools reflect the structure and culture of the society as a whole. As long as we live in a class society then the influence of social class will be felt in the schools, determining the kinds of education children receive and the results they obtain from them. Thus in order to minimize the effects of social class in the schools we would somehow have to diminish the salience of social class in the world outside school rather than the other way around. It is therefore not surprising that comprehensivization does not seem to be bringing the classless society any nearer.

There is a great deal of truth in this argument. And there is certainly something in Corwin's assertion that pressure for educational reform comes from those who are afraid of more radical social structural change.[4] For it is easier to urge more equality of opportunity in the winning of prizes than to increase the number of prizes or abolish that system of rewards altogether.

Yet to say that our educational system reflects the class nature of our society, and that none of the educational reforms so far undertaken have made much impact on class inequalities,[5] is not to say that the educational system *could* not be used as a mechanism for social change. Anderson has pointed out that, over the generations, a substantial redistribution of personnel in the occupational structure *could* be effected through education but only if *extra* educational opportunity were made available to those social groups who had formerly been deprived of it.[6] In other words if, for example, we wished to increase the rates of social mobility in this society, this could not be successfully accomplished merely by moving some of the barriers to success for working-class children. It would be necessary in addition to give those children *more* educational opportunity than their middle-class counterparts in order to overcome the remaining handicaps such as low educational motivation, linguistic deprivation and so on.[7] Thus while education *is* usually a dependent variable, reflecting rather than affecting class society, this does not mean that some social change could not be affected through educational innovation.[8]

Now if it is possible to conceive of ways in which educational changes could bring about other social changes, and if one can generalize from the case of Cherry Dale School, there remains only one interpretation of the results of this study. There must be something wrong with the theory presented in *Chapter 1*. For this caricature of the arguments that comprehensive schools will somehow produce the 'Fairer Society' has simply not been substantiated empirically.

I suggest that the flaw lies in the fifth proposition, a statement which we have so far left unquestioned. Is it true, as so many educationalists assume, that '*Under a comprehensive system of secondary education early selection does not occur to such a great extent.*' Many people would argue that it is, in fact, true by definition, for a comprehensive school is not a selective school. It is a defining criterion of comprehensive schools that 'all children from a given area, regardless of ability, will go to them.'[9]

Now provided that they are not creamed and that the division into areas does not itself represent some form of selection – both, of course, conditions which are uncommon at present – then comprehensive schools are *in this respect* not selective schools. But if comprehensive schools do not select their *intake* this does not mean that they have abolished or even diminished early selection. Selection and the consequent differentiation of courses still occurs under the comprehensive system, children are not sent to different *schools* but the sheep are still sorted from the goats.

For, as we have seen, the majority of comprehensive schools are streamed. And, as Young and Armstrong point out,

When children are placed in streams at the age of eleven or thirteen or fourteen, whether this is done on the basis of an informal Eleven-Plus, making use of intelligence as well as tests of achievement, or by any other criterion, the act of streaming is an act of selection. It may operate in very much the same way as selection at eleven for grammar and modern schools, except that the selection, all within the comprehensive school, is much more concealed from the public, being in the hands of the teachers.[10]

Nor is there any evidence that transfer between streams is facilitated by the organisation of the typical comprehensive school[11] for often widely different courses begin at the age of eleven or twelve and it is difficult to see how children can transfer after two or more years without suffering.

But an even more dramatic manifestation of early selection is still apparent in areas which have 'gone comprehensive'. For, of course, many children have been sorted before they even enter the comprehensive secondary schools. Jackson concluded from a recent survey of urban junior schools that one child in every two is already streamed before he leaves the infant department, three in four are streamed by the age of seven, and by eleven streaming is almost universal.[12] Thus children enter their secondary schools already knowing how they have been defined by the educational system and probably behaving accordingly.[13] The self-fulfilling prophecy of educational selection has been working itself out for years in the primary schools (also more or less 'comprehensive' with regard to intake) and the streamed secondary schools merely carry on the same process.

So it is a naïve optimist who would hope that comprehensivization means abolition of early selection. For in order to produce any of the effects supposed to result from abolition of selection it would be quite insufficient merely to proceed with a programme for 'comprehensive' reorganization. In the first place selection in the primary schools would have to be abolished, for, as the advisers to the Plowden Committee realized,[14] the rot sets in long before the age of eleven, significant educational reform must start at the bottom of the educational scale. In the second place, *if* we wish to overcome the effects of early selection then we must abolish streaming in the comprehensive schools.[15] For this form of selection has all the implications and all the consequences of segregation into separate schools.

But this raises again the question of the functions of the educational system and its relationship with the whole society. For clearly the schools serve not only to provide children with a relatively uniform socialization – to teach them aspects of a *common* culture – but also to provide them with *differential* socialization. It is through the educational system that selection and differential training for major adult roles are effected. And while the burden of distribution of personnel in the occupational structure lies in the schools they will be unable to avoid selection and segregation.

It has often been noted that while the separate schools of the tripartite system continue to 'feed' different occupational levels one cannot hope for 'parity of esteem' and, given the political priorities of most administrations, parity of material conditions is very unlikely.[16] Yet it is perhaps not generally realized that this remains true under a 'comprehensive' system. For, while the different academic streams are 'feeding' different occupational rivers, prestige and resources will be diverted accordingly And in order to accomplish this selection most precisely the processes of evaluation and differential training will begin early in secondary school life. For, even in those few schools where formal streaming does not begin in the first year, evaluation grading and sorting are going on all the time.[17] To this extent early selection is not being avoided and the hoped for consequences of comprehensivization cannot possibly be achieved.

Now William Taylor has pointed out that the most basic case to be made out for reform of the tripartite system is not on 'educational' or 'social' but moral and political grounds. It is, as we have seen in *Chapter 1*, a question of *justice*. For 'we no longer possess a criterion which will legitimise early selection, allocation and the subsequent differentiation',[18] no criterion is accepted as just. Yet the so-called 'comprehensive' education which is currently replacing tripartite does not represent an. abolition of this unjust selection. Selection, as we have seen, still occurs within the comprehensive schools yet it is partly concealed from the public. Under these circumstances discrimination and injustice may well continue unnoticed, for, as Young and Brandis have pointed out, 'It will become more difficult to determine how much is spent on whom. At least we know that more is spent on the grammar school pupil – the accounts will be obscured in the comprehensive school'.[19] In the comprehensive school selection, allocation and differentiation still occur but are given 'a *prima facie* rationality which will make it more difficult for the denied to complain. We must accept the point that the educational system can produce only minimal changes in the world of work and that while it accepts the task of being a selection agency for occupation, it is crippled in its wider social functions'.[20]

But, if early selection is an inevitable feature of any educational system which functions to allocate individuals to positions in the occupational structure, and if educational systems have always served as selection agencies for occupation, does not this bring us back to the second interpretation suggested above? Does it not imply that social change cannot be effected through educational reform, for the schools must always remain handmaidens of the occupational structure?

I would like to suggest that this is not necessarily the case. For it *is* possible to conceive of a school system which is freed of the distortions imposed by the selective function. Surely if we are to dream about Utopias (something which the proponents of 'comprehensive' reform have certainly been doing) then we must be much more imaginative. There is no point in tinkering with the type of selection which occurs in the schools, no point in replacing tripartite schools by schools which are no more than 'multilateral'. If we are to produce any change at all we must completely free the schools of their function as selection agencies for occupation.

But *could* a non-selective school system be devised?

NOTES

1 Howard, A. E., 'Some Methods of Organizing a Comprehensive School', in *Inside the Comprehensive School*, National Union of Teachers, Schoolmaster Publishing Co., London, 1960, p. 25.

2 For the classic statement on the importance of neighbourhood context see Rogoff, Natalie, 'Local Social Structure and Educational Selection' in Halsey, A. H., *et al.*, (Eds.), *Education, Economy and Society*, Free Press, 1961, pp. 243–4. And for the study of the impact of neighbourhood context on the comprehensive school see Eggleston, S. John, 'How Comprehensive is the Leicestershire Plan', *New Society*, (23 March 1965).

3 Warner, W. Lloyd, Havinghurst, R. J., and Loeb, Martin B., *Who Shall be Educated*, N.Y. Harper, 1944.

4 See above, *Chapter 6*, note 31.

5 For a good summary of the way in which the 1944 reforms failed to abolish class differentials in educational attainment see Little, Alan, and Westergaard, John, 'The Trend of Class Differentials in Educational Opportunity', *British Journal of Sociology*, XV (1964), pp. 301–15.

6 Anderson, C. Arnold, 'A Sceptical Note on Education and Mobility', in Halsey, A. H., *et al, op. cit.*, p. 164–5.

7 For a useful summary of the variables intervening between social class and educational success and the relevant literature see Lawton, Denis, *Social Class, Language and Education*, Routledge, 1967, Chapter One.

8 It requires no more than an excursion into science fiction to see how important education *could* be in producing a different world. See for just one example Young, Michael, *The Rise of the Meritocracy*, Penguin, 1961.

9 Savage, Sir Graham, 'The Comprehensives – A Closer Look', *The Times*, (April 1965).

10 Young, Michael, and Armstrong, Michael, in *Where*, Supplement Five (Autumn 1965), p. 3.

11 In the L.C.C. publication, *London Comprehensive Schools* (1961) there is data from selected schools from which one can calculate an average transfer rate of about 10 per cent. But of course these schools had been picked as examples and the data is therefore liable to be heavily biased in favour of high rates of transfer. The staff at Cherry Dale school were unable to assist me in computing transfer rates.

12 Jackson, Brian, *Streaming: An Education System in Miniature*, Routledge, 1964.

13 The reciprocal effect of performance on teacher-evaluation and teacher-evaluation on self-definition and hence performance is discussed more fully in *Chapter Four* above.

14 *Children and Their Primary Schools*, H.M.S.O. (1967).

15 Of course many advocates of comprehensive reform are also concerned to see the abolition of streaming. For a recent overview see Yates, A., (Ed.), *Grouping in Education*, Wiley, 1966.

16 See Banks, O., *Parity and Prestige in English Education*, Routledge, 1955, and Taylor, W., *The Secondary Modern School*, Faber, 1963, especially Chapter Three.

17 I have, for example, observed classes in which teachers have arranged the desks into ability groups treating each according to its supposed capacity.

18 'Family School and Society' in Craft, Maurice, *et al.*, *Linking Home and School*, Longmans, 1967, p. 233.

19 Young, Douglas, and Brandis, Walter, 'Two Types of Streaming and Their Probable Application in Comprehensive Schools', *Bulletin*, Journal of London University Institute of Education, XI (Spring 1967), p. 16.

20 *Ibid.*

8

Epilogue

According to my lights, a last chapter should resemble a primitive orgy after harvest. The work may have come to an end but the worker cannot let go all at once. He is still full of energy that will fester if it cannot find an outlet. Accordingly he is allowed a time of licence, when he may say all sorts of things he would think twice before saying in more sober moments, when he is no longer bound by logic and evidence but free to speculate.[1]

If I have had any success in what I set out to do in this book, the reader now feels frustrated. Like the writer he wants to find an outlet for his remaining energy by producing a solution. If he has been convinced by my arguments (or had been thinking along the same lines himself) he agrees that the so-called comprehensive secondary school system is not after all an abolition of selection. He wishes he could devise something better.

So I would like to have my orgy out – and at the same time allow the reader a vicarious release of his energy – in suggesting a way in which non-selective schools might be developed. I cannot emphasize too strongly that this is only a suggestion. I do not pretend that the evidence presented in the preceding chapters leads inevitably to this conclusion, or that no better method could be devised. Nor do I intend to produce a detailed map of some new route to the old Utopia. I want merely to show that it is *possible to imagine* a situation in which schools could be freed of their function as selection agencies for occupation.

One way in which this could be done would be to introduce an extra tier in the educational system. *'Schools'* could be redefined as educational institutions coping for children up to the age of, say, fourteen. After that age children could attend *'colleges'* in which a variety of different courses were available.

Some children might terminate their education in these colleges, but others might go on to attend other higher educational institutions. In this way some kind of optimum between the ultimately incompatible aims of equality and occupational allocation could be attained.

For the 'schools', however they were organized, could be concerned only with education, not selection. No segregation by ability need occur at all, for children would follow a common basic course. In addition optional interests such as music, art, sport and so on, could be pursued according to the children's individual tastes and interests. So long as there were absolutely no mechanisms for selection and evaluation such schools could be completely free to produce courses designed to give children an understanding of the social world and equip them for full participation in the political system. The whole internal organization of the school would no longer need to be dominated by the demands of the narrow, and (for the majority) diminishingly important, world of work. Thus the 'forging of a communal culture by the pursuit of quality with equality' and the education of pupils 'in and for democracy' of which Pedley speaks[2] could really be possible.

Of course none of this is new! Proponents of comprehensive and tripartite schools alike have long stressed the need for a child centred rather than a narrowly vocational curriculum.[3] The Newsom Report specifically stressed the importance of education for leisure in a world in which more and more people are finding their major life-interests outside work.[4] Yet none of these fine ideals can possibly be expected to be achieved in any kind of school system which is simultaneously serving a selective function. For even in the secondary modern schools, where a major part of the selection has already been taken care of, the occupational structure and its demands impinge on the curriculum: the schools are for the large part concerned with preparing children for public examinations, the results of which will determine their points of entry into the occupational structure' In these new 'schools', on the other hand, examinations would have no place because all children would leave school on an equal basis with no formal qualifications to differentiate between them.

Compulsory education would not, however, end in the

schools. For all children regardless of ability or aptitude would automatically pass on to the post-school 'colleges'. And it would not be until this stage that selection and *differential* education would begin. Some method of allocating children to different courses would have to be devised which, while placing a major emphasis on personal choice and inclination, did entail some means of 'cooling out'[5] those who aspired to courses which counsellors and teachers felt to be beyond them.[6] Some groups could then take three or four year academic courses up to university entrance level, others might take courses designed to prepare them for entrance to other higher educational courses, others could take shorter specifically vocational courses and still others even shorter general or remedial courses. The provision of grants for those staying over the minimum leaving age would be essential in order further to minimize class bias in educational success.

Now it might be objected that this would not be a radically new system but merely a replacement of an Eleven-Plus by a Fourteen-Plus. However there is a crucial difference between the sort of system which has been very tentatively outlined above and all other systems which have been operated so far. This is that all present forms of educational selection – at whatever age and by whatever criteria – reverberate *down* as well as up the educational system. The Eleven-Plus affects the junior school curriculum, encouraging rigorous streaming and special education for the potential successes. The G.C.E. and C.S.E. examinations similarly affect the organization and content of secondary education. For headmasters and teachers naturally want their schools to excel in these formal 'tests', just as parents want the best possible opportunities for their children to succeed. But under the hypothetical system I have just described there is an administrative gap between the 'schools' and the selection procedures. Children are *not* evaluated on leaving the 'schools', thus this artificial criterion of comparison between schools does not exist. Selection is wholly the responsibility of the post-school 'colleges' and, however and whenever it is operated, it need have no reverberation back on to the *'school'* system.

Such a system might also better facilitate the 'second chances' so often denied by our present schools. For the post-school 'colleges' would be institutions for young adults and, while the majority of students would be between the ages of, say, fourteen and eighteen, there is no reason why older individuals might not enter them to take up either full-time or part-time education at a level intermediate between 'school' and higher education. Indeed a legal right to leave from work for such part-time education (as recommended by the Henniker-Heaton Committee) would certainly prove cheaper than the raising of the compulsory school leaving age.[7]

I must repeat that this is merely a suggestion. A great deal of research ought to be undertaken before *any* major educational reforms are implemented. There is some indication that in experimental schools, where courses are designed to interest the students rather than meet the requirements of an examination syllabus, children show an interest and become normatively involved in school life. But we do not *know* whether the removal of segregation and division and of formal examinations would produce problems of discipline or not.[8]

However it seems very unlikely that any of the effects for which the reformers hope will be produced merely by continuing a programme of 'comprehensive' reform. While schools continue to serve a class society, selecting and training personnel for different occupations bearing different rewards and different prestige, education will be unequal and hence 'unjust'. We *can* choose to accept this fact. If we do this then it is immoral to suggest that comprehensive schools will alter the situation for, if this becomes generally believed, then individuals may begin to internalize their failure rather than attributing it to the injustice of the system.

On the other hand we *can* choose to reject this function of the schools. In that case we must think about building a school system which is more than an elaborate grading machine. We must think about creating schools in which children, freed of the immediate inevitability of evaluation and selection, are free to pursue ideas merely because they are interesting.[9] Perhaps there can be schools with a place for Prevert's dunce?

> He stands
> he is questioned
> and all the problems are posed

141

sudden laughter seizes him
and he erases all
the words and figures
names and dates
sentences and snares
and despite the teacher's threats
to the jeers of infant prodigies
with chalk of every colour
on the blackboard of misfortune
he draws the face of happiness.

From *The Dunce* by Jacques Prevert

NOTES

1 Homans, George C., *Social Behaviour*, Routledge, 1961, p. 378.
2 *The Comprehensive School*, Pelican, 1963, pp. 199–200.
3 Taylor, *op. cit.*, pp. 82–102, Pedley, *op. cit.*, and the Beloe Report; Secondary School Examinations other than the G.C.E., H.M.S.O. (1960) all discuss the distortions imposed by public examinations and the possibilities of a child-centred syllabus for the 'average' child.
4 *Half our Future*, H.M.S.O. (1963) especially Chapter 9.
5 This concept was introduced by Erving Goffman, who drew from the case of con men who generally take steps to 'cool out' the 'mark' in order to prevent him from reacting violently and damagingly to the swindle. See 'Cooling the Mark Out: Some Aspects of Adaptation to Failure', *Psychiatry*, XV (1952), pp. 451–63. Burton Clark applied this notion to educational institutions in discussing the case of the American college where certain courses are used to side-track students who would be unsuccessful on the more demanding courses. See 'The "Cooling-Out" Function in Higher Education', *American Journal of Sociology*, LXV (1960), pp. 569–76.
6 This is no place to put forward a blue-print for the selectors. But obviously the system would have to operate in a way similar to the present practice of vocational guidance counselling where trained individuals assess pupils' abilities in various spheres by means of intelligence and aptitude tests. Perhaps some form of examinations might be employed but the important point is that the selection should not include evaluations from teachers in the 'schools', nor any grades or assessments from the 'schools'.

7 See *Day Release*, The Henniker-Heaton Report, H.M.S.O. (1964).
8 It would seem likely that under the system being suggested compliance on the part of the children would be normative and calculative rather than – as at present – calculative and alienative. They would comply with the demands of the school system because they accepted the goals of the school and because they wished to maximize their enjoyment of the courses offered. At present a minority comply calculatively wishing to obtain formal qualifications while for the majority compliance is alienative, stemming from threat of punishment. For amplification of these concepts see Etzioni, Amitai, *Complex Organisations*, Free Press, 1961.
9 This notion, of schools, freed from the selection function was partly outlined by Floud, Jean, and Halsey, A. H., when they said 'The task of occupational selection . . . would need to be shifted to post-school educational institutions'. See 'English Secondary Schools and the Supply of Labour' in Halsey, A. H., *et al., op. cit.*, p. 89.

Notes on the Operationalization of the Typology of Class Ideologies

The creation and operationalization of a typology involves four distinct processes: initial imagery of the concepts, specification of the dimensions along which they vary, selection of observable indicators, and combination of these indicators into indices.[1] In Chapter 6 certain conceptions of class ideology which are to be found in the literature have been refined and their dimensions of variance suggested. The professional reader may, however, wish to know the details of selection of indicators and formation of indices for the operationalization and measurement of this typology.

The problem of translating theoretical conceptions into operational ones is always difficult, and this is especially true where the 'facts' to be apprehended are subjective definitions of the situation. But in this case this common problem was compounded by the difficulty of communicating with children. For pilot surveys soon showed that it was impossible to use relatively 'direct' open-ended questions to measure class ideology. Questions such as 'What is meant by class?', 'How many classes are there?', and 'How do you think people move between classes?' were met by a large proportion of 'don't know's', blank looks and confusion. The problem of formulating the concepts involved in a way comprehensible to the children was therefore raised in an acute form.[2]

[1] See Lazarsfeld, Paul F., 'Evidence and Inference in Social Research' in Lerner, D., (Ed.) *Evidence and Inference*, Free Press, New York, 1959, p. 109.
[2] For, as Lazarsfeld and Barton have pointed out, operationalization relies upon the existence of a shared culture, a shared body of meanings between the researchers and the respondents. See Lazarsfeld, Paul F., and Barton, Allen H., 'Qualitative Measurement in the Social Sciences' in Lerner, D., and Lasswell, H., *The Policy Sciences*, Stanford University Press, 1951, pp. 166–7; or, as Cicourel puts it . . . measurement in sociology is rooted in the . . . "common understanding of the language" in everyday life', Cicourel: Aaron V. *Method and Measurement in Sociology*, Glencoe Free Press, 1964, p. 23.

It was decided that closed schedule questions of the agree/disagree type should be used, not merely for ease of quantification but also because reponses in this form were easier for the children, almost a third of whom found writing a single sentence in answer to an 'open' question a slow and agonizing process. Several separate closed instruments could therefore be administered with less stress on the children than would be produced by a single open one. This reliance on closed schedules entailed the obvious disadvantage that there is no immediate guarantee that the questions meant anything at all to the children who may have merely ticked randomly. On the other hand, the sheer duplication of indicators for the same dimension which could be achieved by this method should offset that disadvantage. For simple correlation of one supposed indicator of a phenomenon against another gives some empirical criterion of the validity of the indicator. And it cannot be emphasised too strongly that the *only* objective criteria of success of indicators are empirical, for there is no *logical* relationship between theoretical and research language, the link between the two being merely a matter of convention or arbitrary whim.[1]

Eight statements about social class prefaced by 'In England ...' were administered and the children were required to respond to them on a five point scale from true to false. The statements intended as indicators of the horizontal dimension (evaluations of the legitimacy of the class structure) were as follows:

(*a*)   If you have the brains and the determination you can *always* get on in life.
(*b*)   Life is like a competition and the best man usually gets the prize.
(*c*)   The only way working men can improve their lot is by sticking together against the employers.

The first two are 'negative' indicators (the response 'true' locates the respondent's imagery on the right-hand side of the continuum), while the last is 'positive' (agreement registers on the left-hand side of the continuum).

Statements designed to measure the vertical dimension (perception of the shape of the class structure) were as follows:

(*d*)   You can tell with most people whether they are working class or middle class.

(*e*)   We are all middle class really.

[1] See Lazarsfeld and Barton, *op cit.*, and Blalock, H. M., *Causal Inferences in Non-Experimental Research*, University of North Carolina Press, 1964, especially Chapter 1.

(*f*)   People who work with their hands are quite different from those who sit behind a desk.

(*g*)   There are no such things as classes nowadays.

Agreement with statements *d* and *f* indicates dichotomous perceptions and agreement with *e* and *g* indicates hierarchic perceptions.[1]

Statements *a*, *b* and *c* were correlated each against each other and, since the strongest (negative) correlation was between *b* and *c* these two items were selected for the index of evaluations of the class structure. Similarly statements *d*, *e* and *g* were selected for the index of perceptions of the shape of the class structure.

The procedure adopted for combining these indicators into indices by means of 'scores' is summarized below.[2]

Construction of Index of Evaluations of the Class Structure

STATEMENT	RESPONSE (True = 1 etc.)	'SCORE'
b	1	0
	2	1
	3	2
	4, 5	3
c	1	3
	2	2
	3	1
	4, 5	0

Scores for the two statements were added and total scores of 3–6 were considered 'High' while scores of 0–2 were designated 'Low'.[3]

When scores for the three statements were added, total scores of 4–6 were considered 'High' while those of 0–3 were 'Low'.

[1] One item 'The class into which you are born is usually the class in which you stay' was discarded as it was apparently a simultaneous indicator of both dimensions.

[2] This scoring procedure follows that suggested by Davis, James A., 'Locals and Cosmopolitans in American Graduate Schools', *International Journal of Comparative Sociology*, II (1961), pp. 212–23.

[3] The decision where to make the break on each dimension was made in consideration of the empirical distribution in order to ensure approximately half each side of the line. This dichotomization at the median point is standard procedure in index construction. See for one example Glaser, Barney, *Organizational Scientists*, Bobbs Merrill, 1964, p. 11.

Construction of Index of Perceptions of the Shape of the Class Structure

STATEMENT	RESPONSE (True = 1)	'SCORE'
d	1, 2	2
	3	1
	4, 5	0
e	1, 2	0
	3	1
	4, 5	2
g	1, 2	0
	3	1
	4, 5	2

When scores for the three statements were added, total scores of 4–6 were considered 'High' while those of 0–3 were 'Low'.

When the respondents were classified according to their score on both indices the final distribution of class ideologies in the sample as a whole was as follows.

Index of Evaluations of the Class Structure

Index of Perceptions of the shape of the class structure		'HIGH' (illegitimate)	'LOW' (legitimate)
	'HIGH' (dichotomy)	19% Power models	23% Deference models
	'LOW' (hierarchy)	30% Instru-mental-collective models	29% Prestige models

Questionnaire

FIRST, SOME GENERAL INFORMATION ABOUT YOURSELF

1. Surname ....
2. First name ....
3. Address ....
   ....
   ....
4. How old are you in years and months? ...... years and ......
   months.
5. Are you male or female? (*Underline the correct one*)
6. *Please fill in the following sentence:*
   'I have .... older brothers and .... older sisters, ...
   younger brothers and .... younger sisters.' (*Write* 'o' *or the
   right number*)
7. Have you been at *this* school ever since you left junior school?
   .... Yes .... No (*Tick one*). If you ticked 'No', write
   below the names of any other *secondary* schools to which you have
   been:
   ....
   ....
   ....
8. In which COUNTRY were you born? ....
   If you were NOT born in England, how old were you when you
   came here? (*Fill in the blank*) 'I was .... years old.'
9. What is your father's job? (This was accompanied by the verbal
   instruction 'Imagine that you are explaining to a new friend
   what your father does, try to give as much information as you
   can) ....
   ....
   ....
10. Does your mother go out to work? .... Yes .... No (*Tick
    one*) If you ticked 'Yes' say what work she does: ....
    ....
    ....
    Is this full-time or part-time? (*Underline the correct one*)

SOME QUESTIONS ABOUT THE FUTURE

11. When do you expect to leave school? (*Fill in the following sentence*)
'I will probably leave school in the .... term of the year 196...'

12. Have you made up your mind about what job you want to do when you leave school? .... Yes .... No. (*Tick one*).
If you ticked 'Yes', please say what job this is:

....
....
....

13. You have just said what you *want* to do. I would like you to say now what you expect *will* be your first full-time job:

....
....

14. Try to imagine yourself ten years from now, when you are 24 or 25. What job do you think you will be most likely to be doing then?

....
....
....

15. Suppose for a moment that you could have ANY JOB AT ALL IN THE WORLD. What would you choose to be then?

....
....
....

NOW GIRLS ONLY

16. (i) Do you expect to: (*Tick one*)
Have a life-time career?   .... (*a*)
Get married and be a homemaker?   .... (*b*)
Both get married and have a life-time career?   .... (*c*)

(ii) *If you plan a life-time career*, what occupation do you think you will make your life work? ....

....
....

(iii) Would you feel a little disappointed if your future husband spent his whole life in *any* of the following occupations?
(*Tick either 'Yes' or 'No' for EVERY occupation*)

Would you feel a little disappointed if your future husband spent his life as a ....

Yes   *No*

....   (*a*) Ordinary labourer

....   (*b*) Machine operator

....   (*c*) Skilled craftsman (like carpenter or electrician)

....   (*d*) Clerk, or salesman in a store

....   (*e*) Building contractor

....   (*f*) Salesman (like car or television salesman)

....   (*g*) Owner or manager of a small business (like a shop)

....   (*h*) Sales representative (like insurance or estate agent)

....   (*i*) Large business executive

....   (*j*) Professional (like doctor, lawyer)

  (iv) What kind of occupation would you *LIKE* your *future husband* to have?

....

17. Some people think it isn't very nice to be very ambitious and to go all out for what you want. Others think it is a very good thing. On the whole do you think that to be very ambitious is a good or bad thing?

    ... Always   ... Usually   ... Difficult   ... Usually   ... Always

        good   good   to say   bad   bad

    (*Tick one*)

18. Would you say that you are more ambitious or less ambitious than most of your friends?

    ... Much   ... More   ... About the   ... Less   ...Much

        more   same   less

19. Do you think any of the boys or girls *in this class at the moment* are ambitious?

Please give the names of the three most ambitious pupils in this classroom right now.

1. ....

2. ....

3. ....

NOW SOME QUESTIONS ABOUT YOUR IDEAS ABOUT WORK

20. There are a lot of different things you might hope to get from a job. Below is a list of some of these. I would like you to read them through and think about them. Then I would like you to write

a '1' beside the one which you think is the *most important* thing
you can get from a job. When you have done that, write a '2'
beside the thing which you think is the second most important
and so on until you come to the number '6'.

FRIENDLY WORK MATES	......	(*a*)
LONG HOLIDAYS	......	(*b*)
A GOOD WAGE	......	(*c*)
CHANCES OF PROMOTION	......	(*d*)
CHANCE TO USE YOUR ABILITIES	......	(*e*)
PLENTY OF FREE TIME	......	(*f*)

Now if – AND ONLY IF – the thing which *you* think is most
important of all about a job was NOT in the list above, write
this now:

....
....
....

21. Whatever answer you gave to the last question I would like you
now to think about what you *really expect* to get from your *first job*.
Put a '1' beside the thing which you think you will like most
about your first job, a '2' beside the thing which you think you
will like next most and so on:

FRIENDLY WORK MATES	......	(*a*)
LONG HOLIDAYS	......	(*b*)
A GOOD WAGE	......	(*c*)
CHANCES OF PROMOTION		(*d*)
CHANCE TO USE YOUR ABILITIES	......	(*e*)
PLENTY OF FREE TIME	......	(*f*)

22. If the thing which you think you will like best about your first
job is not in that list, please write this now:

....
....
....

23. Now I would like you to imagine that you have to choose
between two jobs, 'Job A' and 'Job B'. Both jobs are a 5 day
week with an 8 hour day, but the conditions are different in
each case. I would like you to say which job you would choose
when the two jobs offer different wages.

JOB A	JOB B
Little chance to use your skills	Plenty of chance to use your skills
Boring work	Interesting work
Difficult to make friends at work	Lots of friendly work mates

WHICH JOB WOULD YOU CHOOSE

If the pay at A was £18 a week and at B £6 a week ....

,,	£17	,,	£7	,, ...
,,	£16	,,	£8	,, ...
,,	£15	,,	£9	,, ...
,,	£14	,,	£10	,, ...
,,	£13	,,	£11	,, ...
,,	£12	,,	£12	,,

(*Write 'A' or 'B' beside each one*)

24. I would like you now to *imagine that one of your friends is applying for a job* as a junior manager in a store. What do you think will be the most important things which will be taken into consideration in deciding whether or not he should get the job?

Here is a list of some of the things which might be considered. Please think about them all and then write a '1' beside the one which you think *will be most important* in deciding whether or not he gets the job. Then write a '2' beside the one you think next most important and so on until you come to the number '6'.

HOW MANY 'O' LEVELS HE HAS	......	(a)
THE KIND OF WORK HIS FATHER DOES	......	(b)
THE SORT OF ACCENT HE HAS	......	(c)
HOW CLEVER HE IS	......	(d)
HIS PERSONAL APPEARANCE	......	(e)
WHAT HIS HOBBIES ARE	......	(f)

You have just said what you think *will* be most important in determining whether or not your friend gets the job. *NOW* I would like you to say what you think *SHOULD* be the most important consideration.

Put '1' beside the one you think *should be most important*, and so on.

HOW MANY 'O' LEVELS HE HAS	......	(a)
THE KIND OF WORK HIS FATHER DOES	......	(b)
THE SORT OF ACCENT HE HAS	......	(c)
HOW CLEVER HE IS	......	(d)
HIS PERSONAL APPEARANCE	......	(e)
WHAT HIS HOBBIES ARE	......	(f)

NOW SOME QUESTIONS ABOUT YOUR IDEAS ABOUT THINGS

25. *Here is a list of ways in which grown-up people could be different from one another.* Read these through and think about them. Now I want you to write a '1' beside the one which you think makes the most important difference between people, a '2' beside the next most important and so on.

HOW THEY FEEL AND THINK ABOUT THINGS	......	(*a*)
THE AMOUNT OF MONEY THEY HAVE	......	(*b*)
THE KIND OF PLACE THEY LIVE IN	......	(*c*)
WHAT THEY DO IN THEIR SPARE TIME	......	(*d*)
THE KIND OF JOBS THEY DO	......	(*e*)
THE KIND OF EDUCATION THEY HAVE	......	(*f*)

Those were differences which some people have thought are important. *You* may think that there are other more important differences between people.

If – AND ONLY IF – the thing which you think is *the most important way* in which people are different from one another is not in the list over this question please write this now:

....

....

....

26. *Now I would like you to think about school for a minute.* There may be a number of reasons why pupils of the same age are in different 'forms or classes.[1] I would like you to think about each of the following possible reasons and say whether you think it is true or false.

(*Tick one each time*)

Teachers put pupils into
different forms ....

	True	Probably true	Part true part false	Probably false	False
Because some pupils work harder than others	......	......	......	......	......
Because some pupils are the teachers' pets	......	......	......	......	......
Because some pupils are cleverer than others	......	......	......	......	......
Because some pupils have parents who take more interest in their school work than other parents do	......	......	......	......	......

[1] For Cherry Dale School 'Academic Streams' replaced 'Forms or Classes'.

Because some pupils
are more interested
in school work than
others   ....

Because the teachers
like some pupils
more than others   ....

27. *Below are some ideas about life in England.* I would like you to think about each one and then say whether you think it is true or false.

(Tick one each time)

In England...	True	Probably true	Part true part false	Probably false	False
You can tell with most people whether they are working class or middle class.	......	......	......	......	......
If you have the brains and the determination you can *always* get on in life.	......	......	......	......	......
We are all middle class really.	......	......	......	......	......
The class into which you were born is usually the class in which you stay.	......	......	......	......	......
People who work with their hands are quite different from those who sit behind a desk.	......	......	......	......	......
There are no such things as classes nowadays.	......	......	......	......	......
Life is like a competition and the best man usually gets the prize.	......	......	......	......	......

The only way that working men can improve their lot is by sticking together against their employers.   ....

(*Tick one*)

28. *Which kind of person would* YOU *rather be?*
Someone who spends most of his extra money on his friends   ......

OR

Someone who saves all his extra money for the future   ......
How strongly do you feel about the choice you just made?
I feel strongly about it – I am quite sure of my choice   ......
I don't feel strongly about it – I am not very sure of my choice   ......

29. *Which kind of person would* YOU *rather be?*
A 'smooth operator' who comes out top of every deal   ......

OR

Someone who often loses out because he is too kind to take advantage of anybody who isn't as smart as he is   ......
How strongly do you feel about the choice you just made?
I feel strongly about it – I am quite sure of my choice   ......

OR

I don't feel strongly about it – I am not very sure of my choice   ......

30. *Which kind of person would* YOU *rather be?*
Someone who does better than his close friends at most things?   ......

OR

Someone who does most things just about as well as his close friends – no better and no worse   ......
How strongly do you feel about the choice you just made?
I feel strongly about it – I am quite sure of my choice   ......

OR

I don't feel strongly about it – I am not very sure of my choice   ......

31. *Which kind of person would* YOU *rather be?*
Someone who would rather stick with a few tried and true friends than be always meeting new people   ......

OR

Someone who always wants to be meeting new people and making new friends rather than be especially close to a few old friends   ......

How strongly do you feel about the choice that you just made?
I feel strongly about it – I am quite sure of my choice   ......

OR

I don't feel strongly about it – I am not very sure of my
choice   ......

32. *Which kind of person would* YOU *rather be?*
Someone who believes in 'If at first you don't succeed
then try and try again'   ......

OR

Someone who admits when he is beaten and tries some-
thing else instead   ......
How strongly do you feel about the choice you just made?
I feel strongly about it – I am quite sure of my choice   ......

OR

I don't feel strongly about it – I am not very sure of my
choice   ......

33. *Which kind of person would* YOU *rather be?*
Someone who takes advantage of any good opportunity
to get ahead even when there is the risk of losing what he
has   ......

OR

Someone who would rather have a small but secure
position than take a chance on losing what he has to get
ahead   ......
How strongly do you feel about the choice you just made?
I feel strongly about it – I am quite sure of my choice   ......

OR

I don't feel strongly about it – I am not very sure of my
choice   ......

34. *Which kind of person would* YOU *rather be?*
Someone who doesn't let his plans for the future keep
him from enjoying the present   ......

OR

Someone who doesn't mind giving up most of his pleasure
now so that he can be sure of the future   ......
How strongly do you feel about the choice you just made?
I feel strongly about it – I am quite sure of my choice   ......

OR

I don't feel strongly about it – I am not very sure of my
choice   ......

35. *Which kind of person would* YOU *rather be?*
Someone who tries to be satisfied with what he has and never to want more ......

OR

Someone who is always looking for something better than he has ......
How strongly do you feel about the choice you just made?
I feel strongly about it – I am quite sure of my choice ......

OR

I don't feel strongly about it – I am not very sure of my choice ......

NOW SOME QUESTIONS ABOUT YOUR FRIENDS AND CLASS-MATES

36. Suppose you wanted to pick some people to be your *close friends* – people you would enjoy doing things with and like to have as close friends for a *long time. Which three people who are in this classroom right now* would you pick.

(*Write 3 names*)

(1) ....

(2) ....

(3) ....

37. If you could pick only one close friend *from all the people you know* would it be:

(*Tick one*)

One of the three people you wrote above ...... (*a*)
Someone in this class who is away today ...... (*b*)
Someone in another class at this school ...... (*c*)
Someone in another school ...... (*d*)
Someone who has already left school ...... (*e*)
If you ticked (*c*) SAY WHICH CLASS:

....

If you ticked (*d*) GIVE THE NAME OF THE SCHOOL

....

For Cherry Dale pupils the following was added:
I would like you still to think about this person you have chosen as your one close friend and say whether he or she is in the same *house* as yourself.

(*Tick one*)

......same house ......different house ......not at this school

38. In this class there must be some people who learn their school work better than others. Please pick out the *two* people who are *in this classroom right now* who you think are best at learning their schoolwork

(Write 2 names)

(1) ....

(2) ....

Bibliography

Abrams, Mark, *The Teenage Consumer*, London Press Exchange Ltd., 1959.

Abramson, Paul, *Education and Political Socialization: A Study of English Secondary Education*, unpublished Ph.D. thesis, University of California 1966.

—— 'English Secondary Education and the Political Socialization Process', *Sociology of Education*, XL (3) (1967).

Anderson, C. Arnold, 'A Sceptical Note on Education and Mobility' in Halsey, A. H., *et al.*, *Education Economy and Society*, Free Press, 1961.

Anderson, Perry, and Blackburn, Robin, *Towards Socialism*, Collins, 1965.

Armstrong, Michael, and Young, Michael, *A New Look at Comprehensives*, Fabian Research Series 237, 1964.

Baldwin, Alfred L., 'The Role of an "Ability" Construct in a Theory of Behaviour', in McClelland, D. C., *et al.*, *Talent and Society*, Van Nostrand, 1958.

Banks, Olive, *Parity and Prestige in English Education*, Routledge, 1955.

Bell, Daniel, *The End of Ideology*, Collier, 1961.

Benn, S. I., and Peters, R. S., *Social Principles and the Democratic State*, Allen and Unwin, 1959.

'Beloe Report', *Secondary School Examinations Other than G.C.E.*, H.M.S.O., 1960.

Berger, Peter, and Luckman, Thomas, *The Social Construction of Reality*, Allen Lane, 1967.

Bernstein, Basil, 'Social Class and Linguistic Development, *A Theory of Social Learning'*. in Halsey, *et al.* (1961).

Blalock, H. M., *Causal Inferences in Nonexperimental Research*, University of North Carolina Press, 1964.

Blau, Peter M., 'Occupational Bias and Mobility', *American Sociological Review*, XXII (1957), pp. 392–9.

—— *Exchange and Power in Social Life*, Wiley, 1964.

—— *et al.*, 'Occupational Choice: A Conceptual Framework', reprinted in Smelser, N. J., and W. T., *Personality and Social Systems*, Wiley, 1963, pp. 559–70.

—— and Duncan, Otis Dudley, *The American Occupational Structure*, Wiley, 1967.

Blondel, J., *Voters Parties and Leaders*, Pelican, 1965.
Bonney, Merl E., 'A Sociometric Study of the Relationships of Some Factor to Mutual Friendships on Elementary, Secondary and College Levels', *Sociometry*, IX (1946), pp. 21–47.
Bott, Elizabeth, *Family and Social Network*, Tavistock, 1964.
Bottomore, T. B., 'Some Reflections on the Sociology of Knowledge', *British Journal of Sociology*, VII (1956), pp. 52–8.
Box, Steven, and Ford, Julienne, 'Commitment to Science: A Solution to Student Marginality?', *Sociology*, I (3) (1967), pp. 225–38.
—— and Young, Douglas, 'Reform of Secondary Education in Britain', unpublished mimeograph, The Polytechnic, London (1963).
Boyle, R. P., 'Community Influence on College Aspirations: An Empirical Evaluation of Explanatory Factors', *Rural Sociology*, XXXI (1966), pp. 277–92.
Broom, Leonard, 'Social Differentiation and Stratification' in Merton, Robert K., *et al.*, (Eds.), *Sociology Today*, Harper, 1959.
Brookover, Wilbur B., *et al.*, 'Self-Concept of Ability and School Achievement', *Sociology of Education*, XXXVII (1964), pp. 271–8.
Buckley, Walter, 'Social Stratification and the Functionalist Theory of Social Differentiation', *American Sociological Review*, XXIII (1958), pp. 369–75.
—— *Sociology and Modern Systems Theory*, Prentice-Hall, 1967.
Burgess, Tyrell, *A Guide to English Schools*, Penguin, 1964.
Campbell, J. W., 'The Influence of Socio-Cultural Environment Upon the Educational Progress of Children at Secondary Level', unpublished Ph.D. thesis, London (1951).
Carter, Michael, *Into Work*, London, Pelican, 1966.
Caro, F. G., 'Social Class and Attitudes of Youth Relevant for the Realization of Adult Goals', *Social Forces*, XLIV (4) (1966).
—— and Philblad, C. T., 'Aspirations and Expectations: A Re-examination of the Bases for Social Class Differences in the Occupational Orientations of Male High School Students', *Sociology and Social Research*, IL (4) (1965), 465–75.
Circourel, Aaron V., *Method and Measurement in Sociology*, Glencoe Free Press, 1964.
'Circular 10/65', *The Organization of Secondary Education*, H.M.S.O. (1965).
Clark, Burton, 'The "Cooling-Out" Function in Higher Education'. *American Journal of Sociology*, LXV (1960), pp. 569–76.

Clements, R. V., *The Choice of Careers by School Children*, Manchester U.P., 1958.

Colfax, J. David, and Allen, Irving L., 'Pre-Coded versus Open-Ended Items and Children's Reports of Father's Occupation', *Sociology of Education*, XL (1) (1967), pp. 96–8.

Collison, Peter, 'Occupation, Education and Housing in an English City', *American Journal of Sociology*, LXV (6) (1960), pp. 588–97.

Corwin, Ronald G. *A Sociology of Education*, Meredith, 1965.

Cotgrove, Stephen, and Parker, Stan, 'Work and Non-Work', *New Society*, XLI (July 1963), p. 18.

Crosland, C. A. R., *The Future of Socialism*, Cape, London, 1956.

'Crowther Report' *15 to 18*, H.M.S.O. (1959).

Crutchley, John F., *Work Situations and Social Imagery*, unpublished mimeo, Enfield College, London (1967).

Currie, K., *A Study of the English Comprehensive School System with Particular Reference to the Educational, Social and Cultural Effects of Single Sex and Coeducational Types of School*, unpublished Ph.D. thesis (Education), London (1962).

Dahlke, H. Otto, 'Determinants of Sociometric Relations among Children in the Elementary School', *Sociometry*, XVI (1953), pp. 327–38.

Dahrendorf, Ralph, *Class and Class Conflict in Industrial Society*, Routledge, 1965.

Dale, R. R., and Griffiths, S., *Downstream Failures in the Grammar School*, Routledge, 1965.

Davies, A. F., 'The Child's Discovery of Social Class', *Australian and New Zealand Journal of Sociology*, VI (1) (1967), pp. 21–37.

Davis, Alison, Gardner, B. B., and Gardner, M. R., *Deep South*, Chicago U.P., 1941.

Davis, James A., 'Locals and Cosmopolitans in American Graduate Schools', *International Journal of Comparative Sociology*, II (1961), pp. 212–23.

Davis, Kingsley, and Moore, W. E., 'Some Principles of Stratification', *American Sociological Review*, X (1945), pp. 242–9.

Davis, Robin, *The Grammar School*, Pelican, 1967.

De Fleur, Lois B., 'Assessing Occupational Knowledge in Young Children', *Sociological Inquiry*, XXXVI (1966), p. 112.

—— and De Fleur, Melvin L., 'The Relative Contribution of Television as a Learning Source for Children's Occupational Knowledge', *American Sociological Review*, XXXII (5) (1967), pp. 777–89.

Dent, H. C., *The Educational System of England and Wales*, London, U.L.P., 1961.

Dickie-Clark, H. F., *The Marginal Situation*, Routledge, 1966.

Donnison, D. V., 'Education and Opinion', *New Society* (26 October 1967), p. 584.

Douglas, J. W. B., *The Home and the School*, MacGibbon and Kee, 1964.

Douvan, Elizabeth, and Adelson, Joseph, *The Adolescent Experience*, Wiley, 1966.

Downes, David M., *The Delinquent Solution*, Routledge, 1966.

Dubin, Robert, 'Industrial Workers' Worlds: A Study of the "Central Life Interests" of Industrial Workers' in Rose, Arnold M. *Human Behaviour and Social Processes*, Routledge, 1962.

Duncan, Otis D., and Davis, Beverly, 'An Alternative to Ecological Correlation', *American Sociological Review*, XVIII (1953), pp. 665–6.

'Early Leaving Report', *Early Leaving: A Report of the Central Advisory Council for Education*, H.M.S.O. (1954).

Educational Statistics, H.M.S.O. (1964).

Eggleston, S. John, 'How Comprehensive is the Leicestershire Plan?', *New Society*, (23 March 1965).

Elder, Glen H., 'Life Opportunities and Personality: Some Consequences of Stratified Secondary Education in Great Britain', *Sociology of Education*, XXXVIII (3) (1965), pp. 173–202.

Empey, L. T., 'Social Class and Occupational Aspiration: A Comparison of Absolute and Relative Measurement', *American Sociological Review* (1956), pp. 703–9.

Eppel, E. M., and Eppel, M., 'Teenage Idols', *New Society*, LX (21 November 1963).

Etzioni, Amitai, *Complex Organizations*, Free Press, 1961.

Eysenck, H. J., *Uses and Abuses of Psychology*, Penguin, 1953.

Faris, R. E. L., 'The Ability Dimension in Human Society', *American Sociological Review*, XXVI (1961), pp. 835–43.

Floud, Jean, Halsey, A. H., and Martin, F. M., *Social Class and Educational Opportunity*, Heinemann, 1956.

—— and Halsey, A. H., 'English Secondary Schools and the Supply of Labour', in Halsey *et al.* (1961), pp. 80–92.

———— 'Social Class, Intelligence Tests and Selection for Secondary Schools' in Halsey *et al.* (1961), pp. 209–15.

Ford, Julienne, and Box, Steven, 'Sociological Theory and Occupational Choice', *Sociological Review*, XV (3) (1967), pp. 287–99.

—— et al., 'Functional Autonomy, Role Distance and Social Class', *British Journal of Sociology*, XVIII (4) (1967), pp. 370–81.

Freeston, P. M., 'Children's Conceptions of Adult Life', unpublished M.A. Thesis, London (1945).

Galler, E. H., 'Influence of Social Class on Children's Choices of Occupation', Elementary School Journal, LI (1951), pp. 439–45.

Giddens, A., and Holloway, S. W. F., 'Profiting from a Comprehensive School: A Critical Comment', British Journal of Sociology, XVI (4) (1965), 351–3.

Ginzberg, Eli, et al., Occupational Choice: An Approach to General Theory, Columbia U.P., 1951.

Glaser, Barney, Organizational Scientists, Bobbs Merrill, 1964, p. 11.

Goffman, Erving, 'Cooling the Mark Out: Some Aspects of Adaptation to Failure', Psychiatry, XV (1952), pp. 451–63.

—— 'Role Distance' in Encounters, Bobbs Merrill, 1961, pp. 132–43.

Goldthorpe, John H., and Lockwood, David, 'Affluence and the British Class Structure', Sociological Review, II (1963), pp. 133–63.

Gross, Neil, Mason, N. S., and McEachern, A. W., Explorations in Role Analysis, Wiley, 1958.

Grunes, Willa F., 'Looking at Occupations', Journal of Abnormal and Social Psychology, LIV (1957), p. 86.

Gunn, B., 'Children's Conceptions of Occupational Prestige', Personnel and Guidance Journal, XLII (1964), pp. 558–63.

Hall, J. R., and Moser, C. A., 'The Social Grading of Occupations' in David Glass (Ed.), Social Mobility in Britain, London (1953).

Halsey, A. H., Floud, Jean, and Anderson, C. Arnold, Education Economy and Society, Free Press, 1961.

Hamilton, R. F., 'The Marginal Middle Class: A Reconsideration', American Sociological Review, XXXI (1966), pp. 192–9.

Hargreaves, David H., Social Relations in a Secondary School, Routledge, 1967.

'Henniker-Heaton Report', Day Release, H.M.S.O. (1964).

Heraud, B. J., 'Social Class and the New Towns', Urban Studies, V (1), (1968), pp. 33–58.

Himmelweit, Hilda, Halsey, A. H., and Oppenheim, A. N., 'The Views of Adolescents on Some Aspects of the Class Structure', British Journal of Sociology, III (2) (1952), pp. 148–72.

H.M.S.O., The Primary School (1945).

Hodgkins, B. J., and Parr, A., 'Educational and Occupational Aspirations Among Rural and Urban Male Adolescents in Alberta', Alberta Journal of Educational Research, XI (1965), pp. 255–62.

Hoggart, Richard, The Uses of Literacy, Pelican, 1958.

Hollingshead, August, Elmtown's Youth, Wiley, 1949.

Holloway, R. G., and Berreman, R. V., 'The Educational and Occupational Aspirations and Plans of Negro and White Male

Elementary School Students', *Pacific Sociological Review*, II (2) (1959), pp. 56–60.

Holly, D. N., 'Profiting from a Comprehensive School: Class, Sex and Ability', *British Journal of Sociology*, XVI (4) (1965).

Homans, George C., *Social Behaviour: Its Elementary Forms*, Routledge, 1961.

—— 'Fundamental Social Processes' in Smelser, N. J., *Sociology*, Wiley, 1967, p. 64.

Hood, H. B., 'Occupational Preferences of Secondary Modern School Children', *Educational Review*, IV (1951–2), pp. 55–64.

Horobin, Gordon, Oldman, David, and Bytheway, Bill, 'The Social Differentiation of Ability', *Sociology*, I (2) (1967), pp. 113–29.

Howard, A. E., 'Some Methods of Organising a Comprehensive School' in National Union of Teachers' *Inside the Comprehensive School*, Schoolmaster Publishing Co., 1960.

Hyman, Herbert H., *Survey Design and Analysis*, Glencoe Free Press, 1955.

Jackson, Brian, *Streaming: An Educational System in Miniature*, Routledge, 1964.

—— and Marsden, Dennis, *Education and the Working Class*, Routledge, 1962.

Jahoda, Gustav, 'Social Class Attitudes and Levels of Occupational Aspiration in Secondary Modern School Leavers', *British Journal of Psychology*, XLIV (1953), pp. 95–107.

Kahan, Michael, *et al.*, 'On the Analytical Division of Social Class', *British Journal of Sociology*, XVII (2) (1966), p. 124.

Kahl, J. A., *The American Class Structure*, Holt, Rinehart and Winston, 1965.

Katz, Elihu, and Lazarsfeld, Paul F., *Personal Influence*, Glencoe, 1955.

Keil, E. T., *et al.*, 'Youth and Work, Problems and Perspectives', *Sociological Review*, XIV (1966), pp. 120–9.

Kenkel, W. F., 'The Relationship between Status Consistency and Politico-Economic Attitudes', *American Sociological Review*, XXI (2) (1956), pp. 365–8.

Kuhn, Manford H., and McPartland, Thomas, 'An Empirical Investigation of Self-Attitudes', *American Sociological Review*, XIX (1954), pp. 68–76.

Kuvlesky, William P., and Bealer, Robert C., 'A Clarification of the Concept of "Occupational Choice"', *Rural Sociology*, XXXI (3) (1966), pp. 266–7.

Labour Party, *Signposts for the Sixties*, London, 1961.

Lawton, Denis, *Social Class, Language and Education*, Routledge, 1968.

Lazarsfeld, Paul F., 'Evidence and Inference in Social Research' in Lerner, D. (Ed.), *Evidence and Inference*, Free Press, 1959.

—— and Barton, Allen H., 'Qualitative Measurements in the Social Sciences' in Lerner, D., and Lasswell, H., (Eds.), *The Policy Sciences*, Stanford University Press, 1951, pp. 166–7.

—— 'Interpretation of Statistical Relationships as a Research Operation' in Lazarsfeld, P. F., and Rosenberg, Morris, *The Language of Social Research*, Free Press, 1955, pp. 115–25.

Lenski, Gerhard, 'Status Crystallisation: A Non-Vertical Dimension of Social Status', *American Sociological Review*, XIX (1954), p. 405.

Lewis, Lionel S., 'Class Consciousness and Inter-Class Sentiments', *Sociological Quarterly*, VI (1965), pp. 325–38.

Lichtheim, George, 'The Concept of Ideology' in Nadel, George H., *Studies in the Philosophy of History*, Harper, 1965.

Little, Alan, and Westergaard, John, 'The Trend of Class Differentials in Educational Opportunity', *British Journal of Sociology*, XV (1964), pp. 301–15.

Liversidge, William 'Life Chances', *Sociological Review*, X (1962), pp. 17–34.

Lockwood, David, 'Sources of Variation in Working Class Images of Society', *Sociological Review*, XIV (3) (1966), p. 252.

London County Council, *London Comprehensive Schools*, L.C.C., 1961.

—— *London Comprehensive Schools, 1966*, L.C.C., 1967.

Lundberg, George A., *Foundations of Sociology*, MacMillan, 1939.

—— and Beazley, Virginia, 'Consciousness of Kind in a College Population', *Sociometry*, XI (1) (1948), pp. 59–74.

Mallet, Serge, *La Nouvelle Classe Ouvrière*, Paris, Ed. du Seuil, 1963.

Mannheim, Karl, *Ideology and Utopia*, Routledge, 1936.

Martin, F. M., 'Some Subjective Aspects of Social Stratification' in Glass, D. V. (Ed.), *Social Mobility in Britain*, Routledge, 1954.

Marx, Karl, *The Economic and Philosophical Manuscripts of 1844*, International Publishers, New York, 1964.

Mays, John B., 'The Teenage Culture in Contemporary Britain and Europe', *The Annals*, CCCXXXVIII, (November 1961)..

McCall, George J., and Simmons, J. L., *Identities and Interactions*, Free Press, 1966.

McClelland, David C., 'Issues in the Identification of Talent' in McClelland, D. C., *et al.*, *Talent and Society*, Van Nostrand, 1958, p. 1.

McKinney, John C., 'Methodology, Procedures and Techniques in Sociology', in Becker, H., and Boskoff, A., (Eds.), *Modern Sociological Theory*, Holt, Rinehart & Winston, 1957.

Merton, Robert K., *Social Theory and Social Structure*, Free Press, 1957, 2nd edn.

Middleton, Russell, and Grigg, Charles M., 'Rural-Urban Differences in Aspirations', *Rural Sociology*, XXIV (1959), p. 305.

Miller, S. M., 'Comparative Social Mobility', *Current Sociology* IX (1) (1960).

Miller, T. W. G., *Values in the Comprehensive School*, Oliver Boyd, 1961.

Mills, C. Wright, *White Collar*, Oxford U.P., 1951.

Moreno, J. .L, *Who Shall Survive?* Washington Nervous and Mental Disease Publishing Co., 1934.

Morland, J. K., 'Educational and Occupational Aspirations of Mill and Town School Children in a Southern Community', *Social Forces*, XXXIX (1960), pp. 167–72.

Montague, J. B., and Epps, E. G., 'Attitudes Towards Social Mobility as Revealed by Samples of Negro and White Boys', *Pacific Sociological Review*, I (2) (1958), pp. 81–90.

Musgrave, P. W., 'Towards a Sociological Theory of Occupational Choice', *Sociological Review*, XV (1967), pp. 33–46.

Myers, W. E., 'High School Graduates Choose Vocations Unrealistically', *Occupations*, XXV (1947), pp. 332–3.

Myrdal, Gunnar, *An American Dilemma*, Harper, 1944.

—— 'The Relation Between Social Theory and Social Policy', *British Journal of Sociology*, XXIII (1953), pp. 210–42.

—— *Value in Social Theory*, New York, 1958.

Neff, W. S., 'Socio-Economic Status and Intelligence: A Critical Survey', *Psychological Bulletin*, XXXV (1938), pp. 272–757.

Neugarten, Bernice, 'The Democracy of Childhood' in Warner, W. Lloyd, *Democracy in Jonesville*, Harper, 1949.

'Newsom Report', *Half Our Future*, H.M.S.O. (1963).

'Norwood Report', H.M.S.O. (1943).

Oppenheim, A. N., 'Social Status and Clique Formation among Grammar School Boys', *British Journal of Sociology*, VI (1955), pp. 228–45.

Pahl, R. E., *Urbanisation in Britain*, Longmans, forthcoming.

Pape, G. V., in *Forum*, III (2), pp. 7–9.

Pallister, Helen, 'Vocational Preferences of School Leavers in a Scottish Industrial Area', *British Journal of Psychology*, XXIX (1938), pp. 144–66.

Parsons, Talcott, *The Structure of Social Action*, Free Press, Glencoe, 1937.

—— 'An Analytical Approach to the Theory of Social Stratification' in *Essays in Sociological Theory*, Free Press, Glencoe, 1964, pp. 69–88.

—— 'The School Class as a Social System', *Harvard Educational Review*, XXIX (1959), pp. 297–318.

Pedley, Robin, *The Comprehensive School*, (1963).

'Plowden Report', *Children and their Primary Schools*, H.M.S.O. (1967).

Popitz, H. *et al.*, *Das Gesellschaftsbild des Arbeiters*, 2nd edn. Teubingen, 1961.

Potashin, Reva, 'A Sociometric Study of Children's Friendships', *Sociometry*, IX (1946), pp. 48–70.

Proctor, C. H., and Loomis, C. P., 'Analysis of Sociometric Data' in Jahoda, Marie, Deutsch, Martin, and Cook, Stuart, (Eds.), *Research Methods in Social Relations*, Dryden, 1951, p. 574.

Rawls, John, 'Justice as Fairness', *Philosophical Review*, LXVII (1958), pp. 164–94.

—— 'The Sense of Justice', *Philosophical Review*, LXXII (1963), pp. 281–305.

—— 'Constitutional Liberty and the Concept of Justice', *Nomos*, VI (1963), pp. 98–125.

Reissman, Leonard, *Class in American Society*, Free Press, Glencoe, 1959.

—— 'Levels of Aspiration and Social Class', *American Sociological Review*, XVIII (1953), pp. 233–42.

Robinson, W. S., 'Ecological Correlations and the Behaviour of Individuals', *American Sociological Review*, XV (1950), pp. 351–7.

Rogoff, Natalie, 'Local Social Structure and Educational Selection' in Halsey, A. H. *et al*, (1961), pp. 243 4.

Runciman, W. G., *Relative Deprivation and Social Justice*, Routledge, 1966.

—— 'Justice, Congruence and Professor Homans', *Archives Européennes de Sociologie*, VIII (1967), pp. 115–28.

Samuel, R., 'The Deference Voter', *New Left Review*, (January 1960).

Savage, Graham, 'The Comprehensives – A Closer Look', *The Times*, (April 1965).

Scheff, Thomas J., 'Towards a Sociological Model of Consensus', *American Sociological Review*, XXXII (1967), pp. 32–46.

Schwarzweller, Harry K., 'Values and Occupational Choice', *Social Forces*, XXXIX (1960), p. 20.

Sewell, William H., *et al.*, 'Social Status and Educational and Occupational Aspiration', *American Sociological Review*, XXII (1957), pp. 67–73.

—— and Orenstein, A. M., 'Community of Residence and Occupational Choice', *American Journal of Sociology*, LXX (1965), pp. 551–63.

Sherif, Carolyn W., 'Self-Radius and Goals of Youth in Different Urban Areas', *Southwestern Social Science Quarterly*, XLII (1951), pp. 255–62.

Spector, A. J., 'Expectations, Fulfillment and Morale', *Journal of Abnormal and Social Psychology*, LII (1956), pp. 51–6.

Stacey, Margaret, *Tradition and Change*, Oxford U.P., 1960.

Stephenson, Richard M., 'Mobility Orientation and Stratification of One Thousand Ninth Graders', *American Sociological Review*, XXII (1957), pp. 204–12.

—— 'Realism of Vocational Choice: A Critique and an Example', *Personnel and Guidance Journal*, XXXV (1957), pp. 482–8.

St. John, Nancy Hoyt, 'The Effects of Segregation on the Aspirations of Negro Youth', *Harvard Educational Review*, XXXVI (3) (1966), pp. 284–94.

Stouffer, Samuel A., *et al.*, *The American Soldier*, Vol. I, Princeton U.P., 1949.

Sugarman, Barry N., 'Social Class and Values as Related to Achievement and Conduct in School', *Sociological Review*, XIV (3) (1966), pp. 287–301.

Swift, D. F., 'Meritocratic and Social Class Selection at Age Eleven', *Educational Research*, III (1) (1965), pp. 65–73.

Tawney, R. H., *Equality*, New York, 1931.

Taylor, William, *The Secondary Modern School*, Faber, 1963.

—— 'Family School and Society' in Craft, Maurice *et al.*, *Linking Home and School*, Longmans, 1967.

—— 'Secondary Reorganisation and the Transition from School to Work' in *Aspects of Education*, University of Hull, V (1967), pp. 89–99.

Touraine, Alain, *La Conscience Ouvrière*, Ed. du Seuil, Paris, 1966.

Townsend, Peter, 'The Argument for Comprehensive Schools', *Comprehensive Education*, 1 (1965).

Turner, Ralph H., 'Modes of Social Ascent Through Education: Sponsored and Contest Mobility', *American Sociological Review* (1960), reprinted in Halsey, A. H., *et al.* (1961), pp. 121–39.

—— *The Social Context of Ambition*, Chandler, 1964.

Vaizey, John, *Britain in the Sixties: Education for Tomorrow*, Penguin, 1962.

Waller, Willard, *The Sociology of Teaching*, Wiley, 1932.

Ward, Lester, *Dynamic Sociology*, Vol. II, New York, 1883.

Warner, W. Lloyd, and Abbeglen, J., *Occupational Mobility in American Business and Industry*, University of Minnesota Press, 1955.

—— and Lunt, P. S., *The Social Life of a Modern Community*, Yale U.P., 1941.

—— et al., *Who Shall be Educated?*, Harper, 1944.

Watson, W., 'Some Questionable Assumptions in the Theory of Social Stratification', *Pacific Sociological Review*, XVII (1964), pp. 21–4.

Weinstein, Eugene A., 'Weights Assigned by Children to Criteria of Prestige', *Sociometry*, XIX (1956), p. 131.

Whyte, W. F., *Street Corner Society*, Chicago U.P., 1943.

Willener, Alfred, *Images de la Societé et Classes Sociales*, Bern, 1957.

Wilson, Mary D., 'The Vocational Preferences of Secondary Modern School Children', *British Journal of Educational Psychology*, XXIII (2) (1953), p. 97 *et seq.*, and (3), p. 163 *et seq.*

Yates, A. (Ed.), *Grouping in Education*, Wiley, 1966.

—— and Pidgeon, D. A., 'Transfer at 11-Plus', *Educational Research*, I (1958), p. 13.

Youmans, Grant, 'Occupational Aspirations of Twelfth Grade Michigan Boys', *Journal of Experimental Education*, XXIV (1956), pp. 259–71.

Young, Douglas, and Brandis, Walter, 'Two Types of Streaming and their Probable Application in Comprehensive Schools', *Bulletin*, University of London Institute of Education, XI (1967), pp. 13–16.

Young, Michael, *The Rise of the Meritocracy*, Penguin, 1916.

—— and Armstrong, Michael, 'The Flexible School', *Where*, Supplement 5, (Autumn 1965).

Zentner, H., 'Religious Affiliation, Social Class and Achievement Aspiration Among Male High School Students', *Alberta Journal of Educational Research*, XI (1965), pp. 233–48.

Index of Subjects

Index of Names

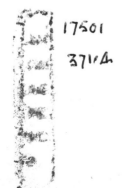